M000312905

 The Jefferson Highway

MARSHALLTOWN PUBLIC LIBRARY

WITHDRAWN

MAY 4 2016

105 W. BOONE ST.
MARSHALLTOWN, IA 50158

Iowa and the Midwest Experience

SERIES EDITOR
William B. Friedricks
Iowa History Center at Simpson College

THE JEFFERSON HIGHWAY

Blazing the Way

from Winnipeg

to New Orleans

LYELL D. HENRY JR.

University of Iowa Press, Iowa City

MARSHALLTOWN PUBLIC LIBRARY

MAY 4 2016

105 W. BOONE ST.
MARSHALLTOWN, IA 50158

University of Iowa Press, Iowa City 52242
Copyright © 2016 by the University of Iowa Press
www.uiowapress.org
Printed in the United States of America

No part of this book may be reproduced or used
in any form or by any means without permission in
writing from the publisher. All reasonable steps have
been taken to contact copyright holders of material
used in this book. The publisher would be pleased to
make suitable arrangements with any whom it has
not been possible to reach.

The University of Iowa Press is a member
of Green Press Initiative and is committed to
preserving natural resources.
Printed on acid-free paper

Cataloging-in-Publication Data is on file at the Library of Congress.
ISBN 978-1-60938-421-0 (pbk)
ISBN 978-1-60938-422-7 (ebk)

Contents

Preface

Although the Jefferson Highway was an important early automobile trail that ran from Winnipeg to New Orleans and was touted by its promoters as the north-south counterpart of the celebrated Lincoln Highway, it has long since passed beyond the ken or recollection of most, including even those who live along the highway's route today. Sensing something of the Jefferson Highway's significance in the pioneering days of road building and long-distance motoring, I set out fifteen years ago to write a book about this forgotten highway. Never able to locate the organizational records of the Jefferson Highway Association (JHA), however, I found that my initial high hopes for the project eventually began to wobble, and after spending several years on it, I finally and regretfully threw in the towel.

A decade later my determination to write a book on the Jefferson Highway was reignited. What brought me back to the project was my discovery of the several archives of scanned early newspapers that are today available online; an abundance of relevant newspaper articles sourcing the JHA's campaign for the highway could go a long way, I conjectured, toward making up for the still-missing JHA organizational records. But I soon realized that tapping and assimilating all those articles from newspapers in all of the eight states through which the Jefferson Highway ran could tie up more hours in my few remaining years than I cared to invest in the project. At last I settled on writing a book that would open with a general accounting of JHA's early pursuit of the entire highway but then narrow its focus to the highway through Iowa.

As it happens, more than personal convenience favored this procedure; not only did Iowa have a special standing as the state in which the Jefferson and Lincoln Highways crossed, but, as I point out in the prologue and develop in the first four chapters, Iowans were central figures in the quest for the highway. Moreover, the availability in Iowa of several important archival collections bearing on the Jefferson Highway made possible a close account of how in one Jefferson Highway state a paved road was pursued and at last achieved but then had its illustrious name replaced by drab numbers.

By thus limiting the book's scope to Iowa, I could also provide (chapters 5, 6, and 7) detailed road guidance for anyone who might want to drive the original route of a sizable portion of the old highway. But here I should clarify my understanding of "original route." In several places the initial path of the highway is no longer accessible, and in other places the earliest route probably can't be known with certainty. Beginning in its first year and continuing in years thereafter, the highway also sustained many small and eventually some bigger route changes brought about by such factors as JHA's initial dependence on the support and cooperation of the communities through which the highway passed and its aim (shared with the state highway commission) to shorten the route and eliminate right-angle turns. I have not here engaged in a maniacal quest to work back through every twist and turn of the early highway in search of its certified earliest path. My goal instead has been to ascertain the highway's route as it took form over its first several years but to note, too, the significant changes of route coming later. The driving instructions that I provide in chapters 5, 6, and 7 are also given a digital expression in a Google map available at the JHA website at www.jeffersonhighway.org (click on "Maps" and then on "Iowa"). I believe that the route guidance offered by my words and that map will take motorists today along a route very closely approximating that followed by early motorists on the Jefferson Highway in Iowa, but I welcome hearing from readers who may believe I've erred in places.

Here I need to point out one more feature of my understanding of the Jefferson Highway that has guided my account of the highway's route through Iowa. Strictly considered, the Jefferson Highway was short-lived, conceived in November 1915 and ended eleven years later when, as of November 1926, numbers replaced names on interstate highways in the United States; thereafter in Iowa the Jefferson Highway was a blend of US 65 and US 69. Yet on some road maps the name continued in usage along with the new numbers for a few more years, and in newspaper reportage and everyday popular usage the name lived on for even a while longer. More significant, the route across Iowa that now carried the numbers of two major north-south highways was clearly the culmination of the efforts of the promoters of the Jefferson Highway; indeed, more than simply the end at which those early highway activists had aimed, it was a vindication of the soundness of their vision and those efforts. To my mind, then, the Jefferson Highway continued to live on in Iowa and does so even today, embodied in large segments of the two numbered highways no less than in bypassed earlier segments. I therefore have not hesitated to note and discuss many features of the highway and of the roadside that postdate the adoption of highway numbers in 1926. Many of the historical images in the book were also made after that date, while the great majority of photographs capture views of the highway and the roadside as they look today.

Many people, most of whom I've identified and thanked in the discussions of sources found at the back of the book, provided valuable information while I was writing this book. Here I want to identify and thank others who provided different kinds of help, including Iowa DOT librarian Leighton Christiansen and his predecessor in that position, Hank Zaletel, for always responding to my many requests for information over a long stretch of years; Jan Olive Full and the late Robert F. Sayre, for their early counsel as I pondered what kind of book to write; Jim Hill, Scott Berka, and Bob Stinson, for reading and critiquing early drafts of chapters and pointing out errors and infelicities; Bob Stinson again, for contributing three photos; my editor at the University of Iowa Press, Catherine Cocks, for her continuing good counsel and encouragement as I pushed on to complete the book; Karen Copp, also at the University of Iowa Press, for her expert preparation of several of the figures appearing in the book; and Sylvia Bochner, for getting the manuscript into the form required for delivery to the press.

Finally, two good friends deserve special recognition and thanks for giving indispensable help repeatedly throughout my struggle to complete this book. First is my photographic consultant, Mike Kelly. Mike provided ten splendid photos, most taken at my request to fill specific niches in the book, and he also expertly took on the huge job of getting all of the photos ready for publication. And then there is Scott Berka, who not only took the largest share of the photos appearing in the book and prepared the Google map available at the JHA website but also accompanied me as driver and consultant on many information-gathering trips taken on the Jefferson Highway in Iowa. Of Scott's help, it can truthfully be said that, without it, I simply could not have provided most of the content and illustrations found in chapters 5, 6, and 7; indeed, without the prospect of that help I would not even have set out to write the book. Because Scott made all the difference in bringing this book into being, it is truly his book as much as it is mine, and I here extend to him my deepest thanks.

Prologue
A Highway to Honor Jefferson

Among the many features of the American scene profoundly affected by the steady growth in automobile usage throughout the twentieth century were the nation's roads. Today, of course, motorists can count on being able to drive to virtually any town or city in the continental United States on a hard surface, usually one of concrete. That was far from reality at the opening of the previous century, however. Then the roads confronting would-be motorists were not merely bad; they were abysmal, generally accounted to be the worst among those of all the industrialized nations.

The plight of the rapidly rising numbers of early motorists soon intensified the movement for "good roads" and spawned many efforts to build specific colorfully named long-distance auto trails. One of the standout efforts of that kind was the campaign to build the Jefferson Highway, an automobile highway running from Winnipeg to New Orleans through the Mississippi Valley. The story of the Jefferson Highway, especially as that story played out in Iowa, is recounted in the chapters that follow. But more must be said first about America's early road problem and the "good roads" movement to which it gave rise.

Beyond the hard-surfaced streets found in some cities and towns, improved roads were rare in the United States in the opening years of the twentieth century; except in a few states on the East Coast, motorists were much more likely to encounter the dirt wagon paths mainly used by farmers to get to the nearest towns or railheads. When dry, these were usually serviceable enough for such limited purposes, but when wet, they were impassable for both automobiles and animal-drawn vehicles. Even for travel between nearby towns, taking the train was once the better option, and indeed, America's highly developed rail network was a major reason why the nation's roads had been neglected and allowed to languish in their muddy condition for so long.

Throughout the nineteenth century, neither the federal nor the state governments had been much involved in road-building activity, a fact that startles when viewed alongside the huge road budgets and prominent road-building role of governments at both levels today. Early in that century, the federal government did undertake to build one major highway—the Cumberland Road, also called the National Road—to connect emerging settlements on the western frontier to the Eastern Seaboard, especially the nation's capital. The project was controversial from the start, however: Was road building a proper or even a constitutionally permissible activity for the federal government? The enthusiasm of Congress to appropriate money to support road construction also steadily diminished, especially as the project got caught up in emerging sectional struggles and partisan debates about "internal improvements." Finally, the emerging rail system soon reduced the pressure to build more interstate highways or even to finish the first one.

Intended to reach St. Louis, the National Road was completed as far as Vandalia, Illinois, when federal funding ended in 1838, and not until 1916 did the federal government resume major involvement in road building. In the meantime, formal authority for that crucial activity was left completely in the hands of state governments, which usually passed the responsibility on to counties, which in turn relied for much of the needed work on even smaller units of local government. Such grassroots arrangements fit a prevailing American ideology favoring government kept close to the governed and recognized that most traffic on roads was local, but these circumstances offered little prospect of securing roads adequate for long-distance travel by automobile.

However, there was plenty of early agitation to improve the roads. The first grumbling came from bicyclists, who in 1893 organized the League of American Wheelmen to push for good roads and even to publish a periodical bearing that very title, *Good Roads*. As the twentieth century opened, automobile owners also began to be heard from, and by the century's second decade, the mounting clamor had ushered in the era of so-called named highways promoted by private "auto trail" associations. The collision of the growing numbers of automobiles with the total absence of decent intercity roads on which to drive them had finally provoked groups of private citizens to try their own hands at securing highways fit for driving.

Far from being fueled only or mainly by members' feelings of exasperation, however, the campaigns of the trail associations were products in the first instance of their members' strong senses of self-efficacy and citizen competence. Full of a "can-do" optimism often noted as characteristic of those years of the Progressive Era, these early partisans of motoring typically didn't propose to build new highways but rather to link existing roads (more precisely, the existing poor facsimiles of roads) and then secure the improvements needed to make them fit for automobile usage. All of the necessary steps—blazing, marking, grading, draining, bridging, and hard-surfacing their trails—they expected to accomplish in relatively short order, so ample was their self-confidence.

Although businesspeople played major parts in the trail associations' campaigns for improved roads, these efforts were not pursued as for-profit undertakings, nor did the associations ever, in any sense, claim ownership of "their" highways, which, of course, remained public property. The associations rejected toll collections for meeting the costs of improving the highways but also recognized that the costs would far exceed what the associations could raise from members. To add to their own contributions, the trail associations hoped to secure support from many other sources, such as county bond issues, volunteered materials and labor, private subscription funds, state and county road funds, and, eventually, federal aid.

The best known, and also one of the earliest and most successful, of the privately sponsored named highways was the Lincoln Highway, which was sponsored by the newly formed Lincoln Highway Association (LHA) in 1913 and spanned about 3,300 miles and twelve states in connecting New York City to San Francisco. Very quickly, the example of the Lincoln Highway gave a huge push to the nascent movement to create more privately promoted named highways. A survey done by the American Automobile Association (AAA) in 1940 identified no fewer than 443 named highways that had been launched throughout the United States by 1926.[1]

Launched, yes, and often also attended by much fanfare, but in fact most named highways did not get very far beyond signifying the hopes of their promoters, and some were outright scams. Of the entries on its list, AAA classified only fifty-six as "principal" named highways, which included all those that had "made a more lasting impression" and "are still more or less in the public mind" as of 1940. Today, except for the Lincoln Highway, the highways on even that select list no longer meet those criteria and have been forgotten by most Americans. All were casualties of a newly defined federal highway system that, as of November 1926, assigned numbers to federal highways and broke up virtually every major named highway into a medley of numbered segments. No longer having any official standing, organizational support, or identifications on maps, the colorful highway names began a fading away that has left them beyond general recollection or recognition today.

High on that list of once well-known and important but now generally forgotten early highways is the Jefferson Highway. Moving over approximately 2,300 miles between Winnipeg and New Orleans, the Jefferson followed various routings through eight states—Minnesota, Iowa, Missouri, Kansas, Oklahoma, Texas, Arkansas, and Louisiana— that had come, wholly or in part, out of the land acquired in the Louisiana Purchase. The new highway, proclaimed in November 1915 but not achieving physical being or definite route until 1916, was named in honor of the president, not far below Lincoln in iconic standing, who had made that great addition to the nation. Touting it as the "Pine to Palm" highway, its promoters also pushed it hard as "The Vacation Route of America."

Following by two and one-half years on the heels of the Lincoln Highway, the Jefferson Highway was directly inspired by the example of its famous predecessor and, in fact, was promoted by its sponsors as the north-south counterpart of the Lincoln. That claim had some plausibility: Each highway reached from border to border across the entirety of the United States, albeit going at a right angle to each other, and each highway could also purport to have opened up a major new transnational avenue of commerce and tourism. True, the Lincoln was about 1,000 miles longer than the Jefferson, and terminating in major cities on the Atlantic and the Pacific coasts, it alone was strictly a transcontinental highway; however, proponents of the Jefferson could counter that their highway also had a terminus in a major port city on another important coast and, one-upping the Lincoln, was an international highway, inasmuch as its other terminus was in Canada. At least four other named auto trails eventually also had routes through the Mississippi Valley—King of Trails, Mississippi Valley Highway, Pershing Way, and Mississippi River Scenic Highway—and the last three ran, like the Jefferson, to the Gulf Coast's most important city, New Orleans, but all four lagged behind the Jefferson Highway in development by three to four years. In sum, as first entrant in the field, the Jefferson Highway faced little effective challenge, at least initially, to its claim to be the premier road running through the Mississippi Valley and the true north-south counterpart of the Lincoln Highway.

Lined up behind the initial call for the Lincoln Highway had been, for obvious reasons of self-interest, various manufacturers of automobiles, auto accessories, tires, and road-building equipment and materials. Even though the highway project quickly picked up a much broader and more widely distributed base of support, those corporate interests continued to be prominent in the support and leadership of the LHA. In contrast, the campaign for the Jefferson Highway had, from start to end, a thoroughly grassroots character reflective of its deep support prevailing among local business and professional leaders and groups located in the cities and small towns along the highway's corridor. These more regionally defined advocates of the Jefferson Highway proved to be as gifted as any promoters pushing the Lincoln Highway; beginning their road-building campaign in earnest in 1916, within fifteen years they saw what had once been merely a line drawn on the map transformed into a hard-surfaced highway, mostly paved with concrete.

By the time this goal was reached, however, at least officially there no longer was a Jefferson Highway, only a patchwork of numbered highway segments, and the JHA had already begun to fade away. The entity bringing the highway to completion was a federal-state partnership that had begun to take shape in the 1920s, had resources far beyond any ever available to any of the trail associations, and was committed not to the completion of any of the named highways but rather to the building of a complex of interconnected highways covering the entire country. To the extent that any named highway continued to exist, it was only as a medley of numbered segments of the resulting new system of federal highways (the one exception was the Meridian Highway, which became US 81 for its entire length). Certainly the partisans of the Jefferson, the Lincoln, and all of the other important named highways could take pride in having initiated and played a major part in the movement that finally brought decent automobile highways to the United States. Nonetheless, the vast number of early named trails, including the Jefferson Highway, began a descent into oblivion.

In recent decades, a rising recognition of the obvious importance of automobiles in the economic, social, and cultural history of the United States in the twentieth century has brought forth not only several excellent accounts of the development of the American highway system but also investigations of some of the historic named highways, such as the Yellowstone Trail, the Dixie Highway, and the Theodore Roosevelt International Highway. The Lincoln Highway has so far had the most attention and study, thanks to the revival in 1992 of the LHA and the publication by the University of Iowa Press in 1988 of Drake Hokanson's *The Lincoln Highway: Main Street across America*, a work whose rich sources included the records of the original LHA. Books about the Lincoln Highway by other authors have since followed, and the Lincoln Highway's well-publicized centenary in 2013 pushed the already renowned highway even further into the limelight.

That there would be a Jefferson Highway was decided at an organizational meeting held in New Orleans in November 1915, but the layout of a definite route came the next year. Now, having reached its centennial year as an actual automobile highway, the old road deserves a closer look at its place in American highway history. How did the Jefferson Highway come to be? Who were the promoters and activists pushing it in those cities and small towns in the Mississippi Valley? What was the situation they faced? How did they proceed? What did they achieve? One hundred years later, what remains of their project? The highway that could once advance a plausible claim to be the north-south counterpart of the mighty Lincoln Highway merits having these questions looked into today.

The problem is determining how best to go about doing so. Several research libraries and the Iowa Department of Transportation (DOT) library have important holdings of materials bearing on aspects of the campaign for the Jefferson Highway, and several other libraries have miscellaneous useful items. Most issues of the JHA's monthly magazines—*Jefferson Highway Declaration* (1916–1919) and the *Modern Highway* (1919–1922)—are available online. Unfortunately, however, the records of the original JHA are not available today and probably no longer exist. In the circumstances, magazine and newspaper accounts published in that period must be the main source of information about the highway and its early promoters.

Thanks to the existence today of online archives of scanned early newspapers, much pertinent information is potentially accessible from even very small local newspapers, many of them no longer extant—an especially great boon, inasmuch as so much of the work of the early promoters of the Jefferson Highway was initiated and executed at the local level in response to unique circumstances, conditions, and problems presented there. Nowhere else are the variegated activities of the hundreds of people involved in the pursuit of the highway likely to be as fully recorded as in those local newspapers.

In addition, these local newspapers can provide an abundance of wonderful "human interest" material. In several small-town Iowa newspapers, for instance, are nestled choice accounts of the first Standard Oil station in Indianola located away from the town's center and out near the edge of town on the Jefferson Highway; of an African American auto mechanic in business along the highway in Osceola; and of the turnout of many public-spirited citizens in Kensett and Northwood to clear by hand the five-foot-high snowdrifts blocking the highway between the two towns following a heavy snowfall. Accounts of this kind are valuable for illuminating the place of the Jefferson Highway in the everyday lives of the people living alongside it.

Relevant newspaper articles are not only an abundant resource but also a widely scattered one, however, and trying to track down and tap all the relevant ones along the full length of the highway over a period of nearly two decades would be a formidable challenge. In order to put a reasonable limit to laborious digging in the newspaper archives and to get on with the investigation, a more manageable alternative is to limn the general features of the highway's history and then take a more detailed look at those features as they played out in one of the states traversed by the highway. This is the approach followed here, and the state designated for a closer look at its participation in the campaign for the Jefferson Highway is Iowa. Subsequent investigations by others could add to the chronicling of the highway's history by focusing research on the highway in other states.

The case for centering an initial investigation of the Jefferson Highway on Iowa is, in fact, very strong. As it happened, Iowans played outsize parts in the successful quest for the Jefferson. The impetus and initial proposal for creating a highway coursing through the Mississippi Valley originated in Iowa, Iowans had already taken the lead in producing an auto trail—the Interstate Trail—between Kansas City and St. Paul that became a large part of the new highway, and the state supplied some of the top organizers and subsequent leaders of the JHA. Even Iowa's location on the highway symbolized the centrality of Iowa in the campaign for the Jefferson Highway: it was the state in which the Jefferson and Lincoln Highways crossed, a matter initially conveying a special cachet to the state as site of the "Crossroads of the Nation" and to which the Iowa State Highway Commission certainly attached great significance in its planning (figure 1). The commission's chief engineer in those early years was Thomas H. MacDonald, another Iowan who proved to be of enormous consequence for the Jefferson Highway. MacDonald profoundly shaped policy affecting all roads in Iowa, including

VOL. VII   FEBRUARY, 1919   No. 1

Where the Nation's Greatest East and West and North and South Highways Join on Iowa Soil in Story County

The road pictured above is part of the Lincoln Highway, also the Jefferson Highway. It is a permanently graded earth road, well drained. It has been maintained for years. Under good weather and season conditions this is a beautiful stretch of earth road. If any dirt road ever had an opportunity to stand up and give good service all the year round and under all conditions, this one had. That it failed is no cause for criticism on the road or road officials. When the picture was taken, there were perhaps 75,000 or 80,000 miles of dirt road in Iowa in just such condition or worse.

Can you picture to yourself, this road tree-lined and with a concrete or brick roadway down the center? Would such a transformation on all the main travelled highways make life in Iowa more attractive and desirable? Would it help keep the Hawkeye people at home and encourage them to spend their playtime and their money within the borders of their own state? Can it be that impassable road conditions may be largely responsible for their longing to escape to the city with its sidewalks and surfaced streets? Would not the lifting of this annual mud quarantine and enough pleasure and joy to life in Iowa as well as satisfaction and contentment to the people on the farm, who, like the rest of us, have only one life to live, to pay many times over the cost, of building better roads?

Figure 1. Dazzled by the joining of the Lincoln and Jefferson Highways in central Iowa, the Iowa State Highway Commission used them to advocate for road improvements. Cover, ISHC *Service Bulletin*, February 1919. Photo courtesy of Iowa DOT. © Copyright Iowa Department of Transportation. All rights reserved.

the Jefferson Highway, and then went on to do the same at the national level as director of the Bureau of Public Roads from 1919 to 1953. At his death in 1956, the obituary published in the *Washington Post* observed accurately that MacDonald had "earned the title, 'the father of all good roads in the United States.'"[2]

What follows is an account of the Jefferson Highway focused on the highway in Iowa that is a product of historical research but also of an enjoyable excursion along the highway's route in that state. The book first looks briefly at the origin of the Jefferson Highway (chapter 1) and the identities, objectives, motives, and activities of the highway's early promoters, especially in Iowa (chapter 2). It next treats the building and paving of the highway in Iowa (chapter 3) and the subsequent displacement of the highway in Iowa and the other states by numbered US highways (chapter 4). The book then takes readers on tours of the Jefferson Highway reaching from the Minnesota-Iowa border to Colo, Iowa (chapter 5); from Colo to Des Moines (chapter 6); and from Des Moines to the Iowa-Missouri border (chapter 7). In addition to pinning down the old highway route and providing tour guidance, these three chapters locate and chronicle the remnants of the Jefferson Highway and its surrounding roadside, documenting the highway's impact on the Iowa landscape. The book closes (epilogue) with brief reflections on what the highway's promoters and builders achieved and the highway's significance both yesterday and today.

The book's objectives are to inform readers about a neglected but important chapter in the history of the movement for improved roads in the United States, to provide a guide for those who may want to explore the old highway in Iowa, and to foster an awareness of early roadside artifacts as well as a sense that they tell an important story and are worth preserving. If the book helps nudge others to carry out similar investigations in other states through which the highway ran, that, too, would be a welcome outcome.

1 ||| Founding the Highway

The campaign to build the Lincoln Highway had a stimulating effect on "good roads" enthusiasts, many of whom soon sounded calls for blazing other long-distance automobile trails. One of those so inspired was Edwin T. Meredith, a well-known publisher, politician, and good roads advocate in Des Moines, Iowa (figure 2). In Meredith's case, however, the example of the Lincoln Highway seems also to have had a transformative effect on his basic beliefs about America's road needs. Long a promoter of improved rural roads, he now saw long-distance intercity highways as a valuable means of linking up all those rural roads that he favored. Great highways stretching across the continent, Meredith now believed, could also be a powerful force for securing an improved national life and even an upgraded citizenry.[1]

When the Lincoln Highway was announced to the world in 1913, Meredith was founder, owner, and chief executive officer of Meredith Publications, a Des Moines firm that published several magazines of which he was managing editor; the two best known were *Successful Farming* and a gardening journal that eventually became *Better Homes and Gardens*. From the pages of the former magazine came many editorials and articles detailing the economic, social, and cultural costs to farmers of being "imprisoned in mud" and calling for state and federal aid for the improvement of rural wagon roads. Several of these articles also questioned the need for long-distance highways crossing states or the nation as well as the fairness of expecting farmers to pay for improved roads that allegedly would be mainly used by city folks out for sporting drives in their new automobiles. Meredith didn't write any of these signed articles, but their publication in his magazine, along with his editorials, justifies the conclusion that his initial good roads objective was the improvement of rural roads mainly for the benefit of farmers.

In contemplation of the Lincoln Highway Meredith must have experienced an epiphany, however, because by 1915 he was expressing and acting on some completely different views about roads. Central to his

Figure 2. Edwin T. Meredith, ca. 1915, founder of the Jefferson Highway. From George Grantham Bain Collection, Library of Congress, Prints and Photographs Division, LC-DIG-ggbain-16011.

thinking now was a conviction that what farmers and all other residents in the midsection of the United States needed most was a north-south counterpart of the Lincoln Highway that would run through the Mississippi Valley connecting Winnipeg and New Orleans. It made good sense, Meredith observed in February 1916, that the "trend of travel since Columbus" had been from east to west, but "the time has come to turn a part of our highway building efforts northward and southward."[2] His projected road he proposed to call the Jefferson Highway in recognition of President Jefferson's farsightedness in acquiring the territory through which the highway would course.

In Meredith's view, the new highway would provide a means of interlinking local roads, and that would give an impetus to improvement of those roads; as he put it in an editorial in *Successful Farming* in January 1916, the Jefferson Highway "will be the backbone of a great system of improved roads in the great Garden of Allah—the fertile Midwestern states." In a signed article published in October that same year, Meredith expanded on the matter of improving roads through linkage: "It is of national importance for a section so covered by a network of public roads as the Mississippi Valley, to have *two* great national highways like the Jefferson Highway and the Lincoln Highway to give the people of these states an automobile outlet east and west, north and south." Of course, those two highways crossed in Iowa, which presumably gave the greatest benefit to that state. Meredith readily acknowledged Iowa's special good fortune but then cited Iowa as offering the best evidence for the truth of his newfound conclusion about how to obtain improved roads: "The importance of good roads is impressed upon the people of Iowa more forcibly by the Jefferson and Lincoln Highways than through any other means. The importance of having any state tapped by a national highway cannot be over-estimated."[3]

Accompanying Meredith's emerging new views about roads—and perhaps another important factor precipitating those views—was an awareness that automobile ownership was rising fast among farmers. As a result, he claimed in an editorial published in the June 1915 issue of *Successful Farming*, "the good roads sentiment is spreading like hog cholera." Farmers were quickly coming around, he thought, to a realization that decent roads, usable 365 days a year, would improve their everyday lives and increasingly were ready to help pay for them. Farmers were even ready to support and patronize a long-distance highway, Meredith believed, opining in 1916 that "thousands of farmers will drive their cars to Winnipeg or New Orleans every season" as soon as the Jefferson Highway was completed.[4] No longer held in bondage by bad roads, thanks to the salutary impact of the new highway on those roads, farmers would be able to enjoy the blessings available to city folks, including taking long vacation trips by automobile.

But all of the foregoing were only the most easily identified and mundane benefits that would derive from building the Jefferson Highway, benefits that were subsumed in the first of two "visions" that Meredith outlined in an article published in 1916 under the title "The Two Visions." The second vision laid out there was a much grander one in which the Jefferson Highway project was perceived as a stimulus to national greatness and a molder of improved citizens.[5]

In this fascinating article, subtitled "Inspirations That Have Stimulated the Organization of the Jefferson Highway," Meredith began his explication of the second vision by identifying the Jefferson Highway as "an expression of the building spirit, the spirit of modern development that is everywhere evident in our cities and rural districts at the present time." Great public improvements take much money, time, and effort but are worth these expenditures because "most of us have an ambition to accomplish something in the world besides gratifying physical necessities." "We are all builders more or less," he continued, and we build even though we know life is short and we will soon depart these scenes. But then Meredith revealed that he was thinking not only of the building of great public projects but also of "another kind of building, a building that is invisible." He elaborated as follows: "We wish to be builders of human minds. . . . And the Jefferson Highway and the cities and the towns and the hamlets and the rural districts that we build along its way, will have very much to do with the texture and the perfection of these millions of invisible buildings constituting men's minds."

In the past, Meredith went on in "The Two Visions," American cities and rural districts, as well as the activities carried on within each, had developed "without much organized human direction. . . . They have been builders of fortunes and of commerce and of things, but they were not so very successful as builders of humanity." But Meredith sensed a fast-growing determination to end that era of willy-nilly development: "We mean from now on to build our cities intelligently, to build our highways in a systematic manner and to undertake all our activities with a greater promise of permanence and of human benefit."

He ranked the just-completed Panama Canal, along with the Lincoln Highway and the Jefferson Highway, high on his list of great national projects that illustrated his thinking about the need for intelligent and focused citizen action that would redound to the benefit of American lives and minds.

Aware of the destructiveness of the Great War taking place in Europe as he wrote in 1916, Meredith called on his fellow citizens to cultivate a passion "for the doing of big things other than war." America, he argued, should "set an example of constructiveness . . . that is not equalled anywhere else but that will be admiringly imitated on all sides." Toward that end, the US Army and Navy should be enlarged and then put to work during peacetime on a "national construction campaign" covering such things as building canals and roads and improving harbors. In this manner, the army and the navy would be "a utilized instead of an unused investment in a necessary degree of military preparedness." But more than merely greater efficiency and economy was involved: "The army should be made a school for young men," he posited, and putting both the army and the navy to constructive uses "is only right in line with modern unity of action and civic development." Once again, his second vision pointed the way not only to increased material wealth and national greatness but, of even greater moment, to improved citizen lives and minds.

Although Meredith's two visions provided an unusual context in which to embed a call to build the Jefferson Highway, his views clearly reflected important strands of thought characteristic of the Progressive Era in the early years of the twentieth century—such things as a new emphasis on improving the governance of cities and the lives of their residents; a determination to end the waste, corruption, and inefficiencies of conventional politics and policies at all levels of government; and a commitment to applying intelligence, planning, and rational organization to the solution of public problems. Meredith's ideas and actions also exuded an optimism and a sense of confidence highly characteristic of that age of reform, features that historian Walter Lord has summed up nicely as a conviction that "whatever the trouble, people were sure they could fix it."[6] Building the Jefferson Highway, then, massive undertaking though it would be, was just one more big project that Meredith could hope would engage the can-do spirit of ebullient and forward-looking citizens, challenging them to roll up their sleeves and go to work and promising a return of benefits reaching far beyond merely the availability for vacation trips of a new long-distance highway.

That era did have, of course, plenty of citizens who would have rejected outright Meredith's pitch to pursue national greatness and uplift through expensive highway projects, holding instead to a smaller-bore vision of road making kept modest in scale and cost and under the traditional grassroots control. If some potential supporters of his highway project might be fetched by his rapturous views, a great many more were likely to be bestirred by nothing loftier than the prospect of obtaining a good road on which to drive their cars. Buoyed by his exhilarating vision of his proposed highway, however, Meredith went looking for allies to join him in pursuit of the project. His quest began in May 1915 with a letter sent on *Successful Farming* letterhead to editors and good roads boosters in many midwestern states soliciting their support for a highway reaching from Winnipeg to New Orleans. When in the early fall of that year he contacted the New Orleans Association of Commerce, he was delighted to find that the organization not only enthusiastically endorsed the project but immediately began to publicize it.

Support for the project followed quickly; the chair of the association's Highway Committee soon reported, for instance, that "almost daily the association receives from ten to twenty letters from all parts of the [Mississippi] Valley concerning the plan urging New Orleans to take an active interest." The steady beat persuaded him that "the people of the Mississippi Valley regard this highway as of as much importance to the North and South as the Lincoln is to the East and West."[7] At Meredith's request, the association then called a meeting to be held in New Orleans on November 15 and 16, 1915, to organize the JHA.

Solidly backing this project, the Association of Commerce sent invitations to 750 state and local governments, good roads groups, automobile clubs, and commercial and civic organizations, and nearly three hundred people showed up. The delegates hailed from eleven states (Minnesota, Iowa, Missouri, Arkansas, Louisiana, North Dakota, South Dakota, Nebraska, Kansas, Oklahoma, and Texas) and were overwhelmingly drawn from business, professional, and governmental callings in the cities and towns of those states. After electing Lafayette Young Sr., a former US senator from Iowa, as presiding officer, the conference proceeded to other business, including approving a charter and bylaws for the JHA and electing officers. In recognition of his leadership on behalf of the new highway, Meredith was named JHA president.

On Meredith's recommendation, the conference's invitation had specified only that the new highway would be called the Jefferson Highway and have Winnipeg and New Orleans as end points; all further decisions, including determination of a specific route, were to be left to the new highway association. This doubtless maximized interest in the project but also assured that the conference would be contentious. According to one newspaper account, "As soon as temporary organization was effected, advocates of . . . rival routes split into two factions and fought over all the convention's business."[8] One faction favored a route to Winnipeg running through Shreveport, Fort Smith, Joplin, Kansas City, Des Moines, and St. Paul, but the other faction sought a more westerly route (the so-called Kansas plan) going through Texas, Oklahoma, and Kansas to Kansas City and then on to Winnipeg by way of Omaha, Fargo, and Grand Forks. The conference could, of course, have looked for a more or less objective criterion by which to make the choice between the contending routes, such as amount of financial support pledged by towns and cities on the routes, the number of people living in those towns and cities, or the amount of hard-surfacing already accomplished on the routes. In the end, all of these, as well as other proffered criteria, figured in the debate, but only as claims made by one side or the other in a process of decision making whose outcome was determined mainly by each side's respective numbers and skill at maneuvering in an essentially political process.

If Meredith had counted on having the new highway come through Des Moines, he must have been alarmed by the Kansas plan's strength at the conference; among its supporters were the largest delegations, those from Texas and Oklahoma. Following a debate sprawling over two days, however, the conference narrowly rejected the Kansas plan and instead adopted a proposal put forward by the newly installed board of directors.[9] This proposal identified cities between Winnipeg and New Orleans that would be "cardinal points" on the Jefferson Highway and left for determination by the board the specific route that would connect them. The cities named were Minneapolis, St. Paul, Des Moines, St. Joseph, Kansas City, Joplin, Muskogee, Denison, Shreveport, Alexandria, and Baton Rouge.

Designation of this group of cities opened the way to a considerable blending of the plans pursued by the meeting's two factions, the prospect of which may be why the board was able to get a majority vote for its proposal. The selection of Des Moines as a cardinal point meant the scuttling of that part of the Kansas plan that would take the highway through Nebraska and the Dakotas, but at least the big delegations from Texas and Oklahoma were assured that the route would come through their states (and the delegates from eastern Kansas could continue to hope—and to lobby—for inclusion). Omission of Fort Smith from the list disappointed the delegates from Arkansas, but their factional allies from Missouri, Iowa, and Minnesota could be jubilant that the new highway would reach key cities in those states. The board's proposal succeeded in accommodating the claims and hopes of a majority of delegates, but much contentious fine-tuning of the route still lay ahead.

When the directors arrived on February 3, 1916, at the Hotel Muehlebach in Kansas City, Missouri, for the first JHA board meeting, they found that nearly four hundred other people were also there, all intent on lobbying for favored routes. In the words of an unidentified reporter for the *Road-Maker*, the board meeting was "turned into an old style town meeting, and they did not omit the band. The most surprised man in the whole bunch was President Meredith, who had gone to the meeting expecting to preside with a gavel and found he needed a gatling gun."[10] At one point during a session described as "tumultuous," in order to maintain control of the meeting, Meredith allegedly threatened to resign as JHA president.

According to the official minutes of the meeting, the board heard sales pitches made on behalf of no fewer than thirteen route variants. The article in the *Road-Maker* noted that "the route north of Kansas City to the Iowa border was quite a bone of contention." Indeed, four proposals were made for this segment, including two that would bypass St. Joseph, even though that city was supposed to be a cardinal point. The matter was finally settled (or so it appeared) by a unanimous motion "that all contests filed on sections of the Highway north of Kansas City be disapproved and that the route known as the Inter-State Trail from Kansas City to St. Paul be adopted" in its entirety.

The Interstate Trail had been under development since 1911, covered over 500 miles of the Jefferson's intended route, and reached all stipulated cities from Kansas City to St. Paul, so it made good sense to incorporate that entire trail in the new highway. By the time the meeting was over, however, the directors had somehow managed to approve two official routes in northwestern Missouri, one going through St. Joseph via the Interstate Trail, the other one providing a cutoff to Kansas City running by way of Cameron.

The highway south of Kansas City was also the subject of clashing proposals: each of the delegations from Kansas and Missouri championed a route running from Kansas City to Joplin on its side of the border between the two states. So heated was the contest that the author of the *Road-Maker* article concluded that "the Missouri and Kansas contingents were there to start another Border Warfare." That calamity was averted, however, when, once again, the directors voted to endorse two routes. They also resolved that whichever route—in Kansas or in Missouri—had the most miles of surfaced road by Labor Day would be declared the main route, and the other identified as a branch route.

The directors designated as branches several other roads veering off from the highway's main trunk. One branch ran from Denison, Texas, to Dallas, and, in fact, a map issued by the JHA soon after the meeting showed this route extending through Dallas to Waco and Houston and then going all the way to Galveston. (Apparently the extension was a decision made informally, because not until its 1926 meeting did the JHA get around to officially recognizing the extended branch route lying beyond Dallas.) Another branch route adopted by the board allowed the Arkansas delegates to salvage something from the meeting. The Arkansans had made a strong case for their route, arguing that it was not only more scenic but also much shorter (by nearly 270 miles!) than a route through Oklahoma and Texas, but the board judged that better road conditions on the longer route justified its selection. Acknowledging, however, that they also "look[ed] with favor on a scenic division of the Jefferson Highway from Joplin to Shreveport through Arkansas," the board added an Arkansas branch to the main trunk of the highway. This branch route stayed just inside the state's western border, following a direct line from Joplin to Shreveport by way of Fort Smith, Mena, and Texarkana.

Three routes lying beyond the Twin Cities in northwestern Minnesota were in competition for inclusion in the Jefferson Highway, but because the condition of none of these roads was known, the directors deferred a decision until the three routes could be inspected. The inspections were made in the summer of 1916, after which the easternmost and westernmost routes were passed over in favor of a middle route going through Anoka and Bemidji. This action completed the initial routing of the Jefferson Highway (figure 3).

Encrusted from the start with tributaries and multiple routes, the Jefferson Highway took on even more complexity in coming years. A JHA route guide published in 1923 showed, for instance, *three* official routes then traversing the approximately 200 miles between Kansas City and Joplin. To the routes running on each side of the Kansas-Missouri border had been added a second one in Kansas—an indication of a continuing route dispute in that state and a measure intended as temporary, pending a final determination of the route. And in northwestern Minnesota, where the two unchosen routes were joined to form a rival highway—the wide-looping Minnesota Scenic Highway—local interests along the western portion of that highway (through Crookston and Detroit Lakes) appear to have touted that route as part of the Jefferson Highway. Indeed, a 1927 publication of the AAA even identified this western road as the main trunk of the Jefferson Highway. Was that an official route change, authorized by the JHA? If so, it didn't show up on a route map issued by the JHA in 1929, but possibly it was another of those routes recognized by the JHA as branches.

The biggest alteration of the original route of the Jefferson Highway came in 1924, when, in recognition of the great progress made by Arkansas in road improvements, the JHA admitted that state to full membership in the association. That meant that, although the route through Oklahoma and Texas would continue as a main trunk line, an additional official trunk route would now go through Arkansas as well. However, the association left the choice of that route to the Arkansas directors, who spurned the existing branch route in western Arkansas (even though it was now mostly hard-surfaced) and instead picked a route that first headed east to Eureka Springs and then dropped south through the Ozark Mountains to Little Rock and on to Monroe, Louisiana. This route was definitely scenic and supported the vacationland promotion of the Ozarks then under way, but because it also undercut Shreveport's long-standing claim to be a cardinal point on the highway, it stirred up very strong opposition among JHA members in Louisiana.

So controversial was this decision about the Arkansas route that it appears not to have held up for long, because the 1929 JHA route guide indicated that the former branch route along the western border—now identified also as US 71—was the main route of the highway in Arkan-

Figure 3. Original route of the Jefferson Highway. From 1923 JHA route guide.

sas (figure 4). Also according to this map, the Jefferson Highway now reached Winnipeg Beach, 50 miles north of Winnipeg, and the main trunk line in Texas now ran to Dallas. Although the second route in Kansas was no longer indicated, several longer-standing anomalies remained: both of the originally designated roads running along the respective sides of the Kansas-Missouri border were still identified as official routes, neither having ever been demoted to branch status, and the original alternative routes through northwest Missouri were also still in place.

In sum, from its beginning to its final days, the Jefferson Highway remained a fluid product of accommodation and inclusion, an amalgam of proliferated and sometimes uncertain or even mysterious routings. It was a highway shaped at least as much by contending pressures from local boosters as by a unifying vision or central direction. The resulting highway, replete with official and unofficial variant routes, loops, and branches, smacked somewhat of another famous north-south highway—the Dixie Highway—but diverged from Meredith's original ideal and inspiration, the Lincoln Highway. Whether that was a matter of concern to Meredith is not known, but in any event, by the end of his presidency in 1916 he could at least feel confident that the project he had started was well on its way toward eventually producing an automobile trail that could be driven 365 days a year between Winnipeg and New Orleans.

Meredith's active involvement in association activities had begun to lessen even before his term as president had expired. Hiring James D. Clarkson of Carthage, Missouri, as JHA general manager in March 1916, Meredith turned over to him the bulk of the onerous work involved in starting up and running the fledgling organization. Although Meredith was listed in the masthead as managing editor of the JHA magazine, *Jefferson Highway Declaration*, he had the assistance of an associate editor and by November had yielded the editorship to Clarkson. Meredith's principal focus in the second half of 1916 necessarily was not the Jefferson Highway or even his magazine business but rather his campaign as the Democratic nominee for governor of Iowa.

Making good roads a centerpiece of his gubernatorial campaign, Meredith discovered that he had been wrong about farmers' support for improved roads and that that cause was not yet a winning issue in Iowa politics. His Republican opponent, William Harding, challenged him directly on the roads issue and rallied much of the rural vote with

Figure 4. Final route
(as of 1928) of the Jefferson
Highway. From 1929 JHA
route guide.

scary claims about the high tax burden that road improvements would bring and the accompanying increased state control over local road districts. In a campaign speech about roads, as well as in an article published in *Successful Farming*, Meredith attempted to refute Harding's charges.[11] Eschewing any further talk about the desirability of building long-distance highways, he argued that improved local roads and permanent bridges could be obtained without raising taxes, without imposing a heavier tax burden on farmers than on city residents, and without losing local control over road projects. His efforts were to no avail, however. More years would pass before a critical mass of farmers, increasingly owners and drivers of Model T Fords, would join other Iowans in voting for improved roads on which to get to town or to take those long-distance vacation trips.

Following political defeat, Meredith resumed his role as publisher, but a four-year sojourn in government at the federal level soon came. This phase opened with Meredith's service on the Treasury Department's Excess Profits Board during America's involvement in World War I in 1917 and 1918 and continued with his membership on the board of the Federal Reserve Bank in Chicago from 1918 to early 1920. Then, in February 1920, President Woodrow Wilson appointed him secretary of agriculture, a post Meredith held until the end of Wilson's term in March 1921. After returning to Iowa, he still kept his hand in politics and even received some "favorite son" votes for the presidential nomination at the stalemated 1924 Democratic national convention. In 1928 Meredith was also mentioned as a prospect for the Democratic presidential nomination. However, after contending with some serious health problems, he died in June of that year at the age of fifty-one.

Although cut short too early, Meredith's life was an eventful one, comprising many honors and achievements. However, one of the most important of Meredith's accomplishments did not come to fruition until one year after his death. The cover of JHA's final route guide, issued in 1929, bore the news of that last signal achievement: the Jefferson Highway, it proclaimed, was now an "All Year Route Practically All Hard Surfaced from Pine to Palm."

2 | Promoting the Highway

The Jefferson Highway's proclivity for sprouting loops, branches, and variant routes was, in fact, a good measure of just how strong and widespread the enthusiasm throughout the Mississippi Valley was for Meredith's proposed highway. The first issue of *Jefferson Highway Declaration* (February 1916) recorded some further impressive evidence of the highway's enthusiastic reception, such as the very rapid formation in most of the states of county JHA organizations, the successful efforts in many of the counties through which the highway ran to secure bond referendums for financing the highway's hard-surfacing, and the Minnesota State Highway Commission's decision to place under the state's "active improvement" the entire Jefferson Highway route in Minnesota, once that route was finally determined. (This last item was followed three months later with an intriguing notice—but no details provided—that "an enthusiasm and activity [for the Jefferson Highway] that bars description has been running riot in Minnesota.") Tucked into issues throughout the *Declaration*'s first year of publication were many more tidbits indicating the highway's high level of popular support—reports, for instance, that the small city of Hampton, Iowa, had raised $1,750 for graveling the highway in its precincts; that a resident of Carterville, Missouri, had donated five hundred tons of gravel (worth $3,000) for use on the highway; and that the Women's Clubs of New Orleans, Shreveport, and Des Moines were considering what they might do to beautify the highway.

What lay behind that fervent support for the Jefferson Highway? What did those enthusiastic supporters expect to get from its realization? Owners of automobiles, of course, could look forward to another decent intercity road on which to drive, at a time when there were precious few such roads available. An even wider support rested on perceptions of economic benefit to be derived from the commerce generated by traffic on the new highway. An expected increase in interstate vacation tourism was often forecast in the early issues of the *Declaration*, both by Minnesotans expecting an increase in summer travel to the "Land of 10,000 Lakes" (a slogan concocted then for promotional purposes) and by southerners, such as Walter Parker, general manager of the New Orleans Association of Commerce, who expected an increased winter vacation trade in his city, thanks to the highway. In a *Declaration* article (September 1916), Parker also predicted that the highway would yield increased traffic in commodities moving to and from the New Orleans port, a rise in property values along the route, and a general improvement in the condition of other roads connecting to the highway, as Meredith had also contended.

Going beyond Parker's generalities, William Polk, secretary of the Louisiana Good Roads Association, provided in another *Declaration* article (April 1916) some data, presumably derived from research, that purported to express concretely the benefits that would flow to farmers, workers, and businesses along the highway. Road construction, he claimed, would increase the demand for labor, thereby also pushing up wages; an additional $12.5 million, spent in the construction of the highway and by travelers on it, would go into circulation along the route and have beneficial multiplier effects; within 5 miles of the highway land values would increase by $10 to $35 per acre; and, thanks to the improved highway and local roads adjoining it, the cost to farmers of hauling crops would fall from 28 cents per ton mile to 9 cents per ton mile. Meredith's defeat in the 1916 gubernatorial election suggests that Polk's arguments may not yet have taken hold among farmers, but his and Parker's claims undoubtedly represented the views and hopes of commercial organizations, many businesspeople, and government officials in the cities and small towns along the entire route.

Yet for most of the residents, enthusiastic support for the Jefferson Highway must have rested at least in part on strong feelings of civic pride and a sense of strengthened ties to a larger outer world. If a new highway was in the offing that purported to connect all cities and towns on a route traversing the United States from the Canadian border to the Gulf of Mexico, who wouldn't want their city or town to be on it, and who wouldn't feel excitement about the prospect of thereby being connected to larger regional and national communities (even an international community, inasmuch as the highway reached into Canada)?

Indeed, even Parker and Polk, although they emphasized economic benefits, thought there was something to the notion of a tie between highways and a longing for social connection. In the September 1916 *Declaration* article Parker claimed that the Jefferson Highway would give a "great impetus" to "wholesome community building" and that through the resultant "united community effort, local community problems will seem easier of solution than before." Polk argued in his article that a long-distance highway served a yearning for, as well as promoted the building of, community by "dissipat[ing] the tendency to become suspicious and timid, a characteristic that always developes [sic] in people when isolated." In these arguments, of course, were strong hints of Meredith's belief, expressed in the second of his two visions, that the Jefferson Highway and other great national projects would bring an improved citizenry possessed of an enlarged outlook.

The rest of Meredith's second vision—about how great projects befit a great nation—was also echoed by other writers in these pages. Fred Wright, associate editor of the *Declaration*, argued in "A Nation of Builders" (June 1916), for instance, that America was unique among nations in having a civilization defined by a commitment to carrying out massive projects of great utility, such as the Panama Canal and the Jefferson Highway, for the benefit of all citizens. In a similar vein, Harry W. Graham, secretary of the Chillicothe, Missouri, Chamber of Commerce, answered the question "Why a Jefferson Highway?" (*Declaration*, April 1916) this way: "Because Thomas Jefferson had it in mind. He saw its need." According to Graham, President Jefferson had envisioned four great national highways, only one of which—the National Road—was ever begun (but never completed). But in the twentieth century, Graham continued, Jefferson's project was, in effect, being revived by private associations pushing to build long-distance auto trails, and, as it happened, the last of Jefferson's four highways to be tackled was none other than the Jefferson Highway. Building it now, Graham concluded, not only would be a task worthy of a great nation but would also give due recognition to a great president by bringing his project to completion. Whatever the degree of accuracy of Graham's historical facts and claims, his surprising argument that Jefferson endorsed the building of the highway bearing his name could only have swelled the enthusiasm fueling the project.

To tap the mounting support for building the highway and to direct it toward obtaining definite results, Meredith hired James D. Clarkson of Carthage, Missouri, as JHA's general manager.[1] A well-known preacher of the evangel of constructing automobile roads adequate for use in all weather conditions, Clarkson also was, in the words of the *Road-Maker* (May 1916), "undoubtedly the leading figure of the country when it comes . . . to inspiring community action" on behalf of such roads. He had been a longtime automobile and implement dealer in Carthage but eventually abandoned that business to devote his full time to the good roads cause as president of the National League of 365-Day Road Clubs. Meredith's personal assistant had heard Clarkson speak at a good roads conference in Cedar Rapids in 1915 and was so impressed that he began to follow Clarkson's good roads work and finally recommended that Meredith hire him. In April 1916, Clarkson assumed the duties of JHA general manager, and it was soon evident that Meredith's assistant had been right: Clarkson was a superb fit for the job.

Totally dedicated to the Jefferson Highway and seemingly indefatigable, Clarkson immediately set out for Minnesota to settle the route question there and spent the next forty-five days on the road. By the end of his first year, moving by both automobile and train, he had traveled the entire route, everywhere very effectively whooping up the highway and promoting local organizations to carry on the work needed to make it a reality. According to the May 1916 article in the *Road-Maker*, everywhere Clarkson "preaches the gospel of DO IT NOW" and, after only one month on the job, "was setting the 'woods' on fire with enthusiasm from Winnipeg to the Gulf." The magazine credited his unusual effectiveness to "his practical experience in road building, his wonderful genius for organization, and his lovable personality." Later that year, reporting on a Clarkson appearance in Donaldson, Louisiana, the local newspaper, the *Donaldson Chief* (as copied in *Jefferson Highway Declaration*, December 1916), found Clarkson to be "a fluent and easy speaker with an engaging sense of humor and a pleasing manner of expression" who "succeeded in imparting to his auditors a measure of his own enthusiasm over the Jefferson Highway project." The evidence was piling up; clearly Clarkson was the right person to take on the difficult task of promoting the Jefferson Highway.

By the end of 1916, Clarkson had taken over from Meredith and his associate editor the full task of editing the *Declaration*, after which for several years that journal's pages were full of reprints or accounts of Clarkson's speeches. Soon finely honed and road-tested, many themes of these speeches repeated and reached the stratospheric heights of those found in Meredith's second vision of an upgraded citizenry following in the highway's wake. Apparently such lofty material, especially when served up by an inspirational charmer, was what roused the audiences and induced them to support the projected highway.

In order to edit the magazine, manage the organization, and stay constantly on the road, Clarkson traveled in a specially designed touring car that contained his office, a Dictaphone, and files (and also served initially as his living quarters while traveling). The new circumstances of his work life apparently caused problems for his home life, however, because at the June 1917 meeting of the board of directors, he announced that "my connection with the Jefferson Highway Association has been such that it has been necessary to discontinue my home [in Carthage]." Unless the board objected, he declared, thereafter Mrs. Clarkson would travel with him, assisting him in his duties, and her travel expenses would also be charged to the JHA. Doubtless recognizing in Clarkson an effectiveness and a devotion to the cause far beyond the ordinary, the board raised no objections.

Clarkson's leadership and promotional activities quickly brought good results. After one year's effort, the JHA had local committees in all seven states and eighty-seven counties crossed by the Jefferson Highway and enough money in the bank to keep the organization going for a second year. Shortly after becoming editor of the *Declaration*, Clarkson reported to the board of directors that his success in securing more advertisers meant that that journal no longer drained JHA finances. Moving the JHA home office from Des Moines to St. Joseph in 1918, Clarkson cut expenses by having the JHA join forces with the organization promoting the Pikes Peak Ocean to Ocean Highway, which also ran through St. Joseph. As of March 1920, the two road groups shared not only an office in St. Joseph but also a promotional magazine, the *Modern Highway*, of which Clarkson became editor and which replaced the *Declaration*.

When the JHA's bank account neared depletion in 1918, Clarkson revived the association's financial condition by devising a new method of assessing cities and counties on the route. Essentially a franchise-granting scheme, his new method included bestowing on the general manager the power to relocate the Jefferson Highway route as a means of last resort for securing maintenance of the highway and payment of assessments by localities. (In January 1920, Clarkson reported having used this sanction on five occasions, all approved after the fact by the JHA board.)

Once the highway route was determined, Clarkson turned to the task of getting the route marked. By 1919, over fifteen thousand stenciled pole marks and twenty-five hundred enameled steel signs were in place to guide motorists. The pole marks consisted of two six-inch blue bands separated by a twelve-inch white band on which were placed the conjoined letters "J" and "H" in black. The steel signs, put up at mile intervals, indicated the highway's name and its terminal cities of Winnipeg and New Orleans and carried stylized depictions of pine and palm trees—a visual representation of JHA's claim that the highway ran from "Pine to Palm" (figure 5). To help give substance to this slogan, road boosters in Winnipeg and New Orleans pledged to plant pine or palm trees, respectively, along the highway approaches to their cities, but to what extent the pledge was carried out by either group is not known.[2]

Another slogan concocted by Clarkson—"The Vacation Route of America"—exploited the fact that, because the Jefferson Highway ranged over twenty degrees of latitude, agreeable weather could be found somewhere on the route during any season. As more Americans had automobiles and disposable income and took vacations, many might be enticed to flee the summer's heat by heading to the coolness of the North Woods, or to escape winter's snowy blast by motoring to the sunny Southland. To promote the notion that the Jefferson Highway was an ideal route for year-round vacation travel and ready for such use, Clarkson organized a so-called sociability run from St. Joseph to Winnipeg and back in the summer of 1916.

Although most of the road had not yet been hard-surfaced, a very large number of automobiles—the official count was 2,773 cars—managed to negotiate all or substantial portions of this long trek (figure 6). Traveling in those automobiles or appearing on welcoming platforms in cities and towns along the route were scores of enthusiastic and loquacious boosters—JHA officials, chamber of commerce representatives, bloviating politicians and city administrators, local businessmen and their wives. All were eager to hymn the merits of their fair cities and join in the celebration of the Jefferson Highway. Frequently heard themes were the highway's salutary role in promoting amity between town and country, between North and South, and between two nations.[3]

Walter Parker was a participant in that first sociability run. Devoting three weeks to the trip and traveling in one of six touring cars carrying New Orleans dignitaries, he sent a message back to his boss at the New Orleans Association of Commerce that he was "getting lots of air, but mighty little rest."[4] So far, he claimed, he had given over sixty short speeches on "New Orleans, the Southern Terminus of the Jefferson Highway." (By the end of his "working vacation," the total number of

Figure 5. JHA used two types of signs: a stenciled "JH" and an enameled steel "Pine to Palm." Photo by Mike Kelly.

Figure 6. JHA general manager J. D. Clarkson (*center*) in Winnipeg during 1916 sociability run. From *Jefferson Highway Declaration*, October 1916. Photo courtesy of Special Collections Department, Iowa State University Library.

speeches would stand at 127.) He explained how he and the many other speakers on this run were able to accomplish their tasks efficiently: "At each town each car stopped just ten minutes. Each of the official cars carried one speaker, who was introduced by the speaker in the preceding car. In turn he introduced the speaker in the next car behind. In this way a programme of from half to a full hour was staged at each town, but no car would lose more than ten minutes. Extra high power cars were provided so no speaker would fall behind his programme time in the event of tire trouble" (figure 7).

Parker was delighted by the reception he got along the route. "Many citizens along the road expressed open eyed amazement over the development work going on at New Orleans," he reported. Interest in the new highway ran high, too: "At every town we stopped [at] in Missouri, Iowa, and Minnesota, great signs reading 'Jefferson Highway—New Orleans, Winnipeg' were hung across the road, and great road maps showing the Jefferson Highway were displayed."[5] So festive and pro-

Figure 7. An escort car in Osceola waiting to guide the 1916 sociability run to Indianola. Photo courtesy of Clarke County Historical Society.

ductive was the sociability run that the JHA sponsored at least five more in the next ten years, including a southern tour from St. Joseph to New Orleans in late fall of 1916 that complemented the summer's successful northern run and a 1926 trek that left Winnipeg for New Orleans during a January blizzard. This latter run was intended to demonstrate that the Jefferson Highway could already be traveled in any season. No matter that in a December 29, 1925, letter to JHA headquarters, Fred White, chief engineer of the Iowa State Highway Commission, had strongly advised against the run, citing the risks facing motorists on any road in Iowa in winter and noting that the Jefferson Highway lacked a hard surface from Des Moines to the Missouri line. In spite of White's worries, the sociability run reached New Orleans more or less on schedule.

Sociability runs were a Clarkson specialty, his gaudiest and most elaborate concoctions for publicizing the Jefferson Highway, but, as it happened, he did not organize this daring winter sociability run in 1926 or even the one preceding it in the fall of 1925. Citing a "failing condition" of his health, he had retired from his position of JHA general manager in March 1922. When the JHA executive committee—no doubt greatly alarmed by the prospect of losing him—suggested that he take a paid vacation until his health was restored, Clarkson said he could see no alternative to giving up the work entirely, because "a vacation would be a rest from work only and not from responsibility, which was the real load."[6] Reluctantly accepting his resignation, JHA hired as his replacement A. H. French, a sales manager for a coal company in Pittsburg, Kansas, who, according to the *Modern Highway* (August 1922), also had "considerable experience in road matters" and was "a real, hustling every-day-in-the-year good roads enthusiast."

Clarkson lived another seventeen years, which suggests that he was simply burned out after six years as JHA's general manager—and no wonder, given the pace at which he worked, the wide range of tasks he undertook, and the many hours he spent on the road on behalf of the JHA. No one had done more to promote the cause of the Jefferson Highway during the early start-up years, and he left an effective organization for his successor. Clarkson had gotten that organization up and running, fostered the full development of state and county organizations, made the JHA financially solvent, and kept it steadily focused on achieving a 365-day highway, a goal that looked ever more certain of attainment as French took over the duties of general manager. Meredith's appointment of Clarkson had clearly been a stroke of great good fortune for the JHA. Indeed, next to bringing the JHA into being, hiring Clarkson very likely was the most beneficial and consequential action Meredith ever took in his quest for the Jefferson Highway.

Clarkson, of course, was not the only official acting on behalf of the JHA, which had the usual panoply of officers, a board of directors consisting of the general officers and a state vice president, and three state committeemen from each Jefferson Highway state. But the JHA was primarily a promotional organization and relied on many others to carry out the cause it was promoting. That meant that most of the hard work of securing the route and financing and building the highway took place at the state and county levels rather than at the central level and spoke to the great importance of Clarkson's efforts to build state and county organizations. At the same time, the burden of this task was eased considerably by the enormous enthusiasm that had already stimulated, even before Clarkson arrived on the scene, the formation of many state and county organizations by local good roads boosters.

Certainly Clarkson's organizing task must have been at its least burdensome in the territory lying between Kansas City and St. Paul,

Figure 8. W. A. Hopkins, founder of the Interstate Trail and early JHA leader. From *Jefferson Highway Declaration*, February 1920. Photo by Mike Kelly.

the terminal cities of the Interstate Trail. Having adopted that trail's entire route, the JHA also took over the organizational structure of the Interstate Trail Association, which had been in place and active for five years and whose experienced leaders now went to work on behalf of the Jefferson Highway. Several of those leaders, located in Iowa, were especially able and effective and provided critical service to the JHA. In their personal features, backgrounds, and road activities they also illustrate the kind of individuals rallying to the cause of the Jefferson Highway everywhere along the highway's route.

As laid out at its inception in 1911, the Interstate Trail originated in Kansas City, continued to St. Joseph, entered Iowa at Lamoni, and then went through Osceola and Indianola to the route's terminus in Des Moines. The prime mover for the creation of the Interstate Trail was Lamoni resident W. A. Hopkins, who remained president of the trail's association throughout all five years of its existence (figure 8). Starting as an undertaker and proprietor of a furniture store in Lamoni, Hopkins eventually became president of a local bank. An ardent enthusiast for improved automobile roads, he chaired the good roads committee of

Figure 9. Hugh Shepard, early JHA leader. From *Jefferson Highway Declaration*, September 1919. Photo by Mike Kelly.

the Iowa Bankers Association and was also a founder and leader of the movement to establish the Waubonsie Trail, an east-west road reaching across southern Iowa that ran through Lamoni.

From the start, many of the Interstate Trail's supporters hoped to see it extended beyond Des Moines, which became a real possibility in 1914, thanks to the enlistment of a newcomer to the good roads movement, Hugh Shepard of Mason City (figure 9). Shepard was a prominent lawyer in that city, also proprietor of an abstract and farm loan business there, and a very active participant in many city and state civic organizations and activities. Working through his district's member of Congress, for example, in June 1911 Shepard had obtained eight hundred thousand young pike ("in the wiggler stage," according to a newspaper account) to stock nearby Clear Lake, and early in 1914 he was one of the organizers of a statewide booster group, the Greater Iowa Association. That group's first big goal was making sure that Iowa was represented by a suitable building and exhibits at the 1915 Panama-

Pacific Exposition in San Francisco. Soon Shepard and fourteen other Iowans were appointed by Governor George W. Clarke to a committee charged with making plans for the Iowa exhibits and raising money to fund them. To raise funds, Shepard and some of his fellow committee members secured $105,000 in pledges through a one-week tour in May of all the larger cities of Iowa. An able organizer and promoter, and well recognized in the booster parlance of that day as a "live wire," Shepard apparently also had a scholarly bent, because in October 1914 he was selected as a board member of the State Historical Society of Iowa (and he was an 1897 Phi Beta Kappa graduate from the State University of Iowa).

Assisted by Hopkins, in January 1915 Shepard organized and hosted a major good roads conference in Mason City to stir up interest in bringing the Interstate Trail through that city. Tapped at that conference to be the Interstate Trail Association's general manager for the Northern Division (an unpaid position in spite of the lofty title), Shepard launched a vigorous effort to organize, improve, and mark the entirety of the highway running from Des Moines to St. Paul via Mason City. Very quickly, of course, his efforts were instead channeled into promoting the Jefferson Highway, but that couldn't happen before he and Hopkins had first secured the incorporation of the Interstate Trail into the new highway. Because their work toward that end showed considerable political adroitness, it's worth returning briefly to those initial JHA organizational meetings in late 1915 and early 1916 for a closer look at their performance.

Recognizing that there were many options for a highway route from New Orleans to Winnipeg and that some rival routes to the Interstate Trail were likely to be championed at the initial meeting in New Orleans, Hopkins and Shepard undertook at once to get as many supporters of the Interstate Trail as possible lined up to attend that meeting. On November 9, 1915, the *Mason City Globe-Gazette* reported that "for the past several weeks Hugh H. Shepard has been busy interesting others along the Interstate Trail, so that a unified movement of Interstate enthusiasts could be made." Two days later in the same newspaper came this update: "A large number of delegates from cities and towns on the Interstate Trail in Missouri, Iowa and Minnesota leave tomorrow night for New Orleans, to attend the Jefferson Highway meeting there. . . . All cities of any size have arranged to send delegates and they have their plans well enough laid in advance, largely under the direction of Hugh Shepard . . . so that there will be no guess work in their campaign. They hope to go down so much better organized than delegates representing any other 500 miles of highway that there will be no chance for the convention to turn down their demands."

Indicative of the kinds of small-town business- and professional men making up the Iowa delegation were, for instance, a Sheffield banker, a Nevada lawyer, a lumber and cement merchant from Indianola, and a Leon newspaper editor. A more notable member of the delegation was Lafayette Young Sr., publisher and editor of the *Des Moines Capital*; earlier in his newspaper career he had been a war correspondent in the Balkans and somehow along the way had picked up the courtesy title of colonel. He was also a former president of the Iowa Good Roads Association and a founder of the River to River Road, an early east-west automobile trail across Iowa. Active in Republican politics, Young had been a member of the Iowa Senate for twelve years, then served a brief interim appointment as US senator from Iowa in 1910–1911, and was held in high professional esteem as a great stump speaker. In recognition of his political experience and skills, he was chosen at the New Orleans meeting to be the permanent chair of the proceedings. That was a matter of good fortune for the Interstate Trail advocates, but it also proved to be an especially challenging assignment, in view of the great factional clash there and the steady attempts of the Oklahoma and Texas delegations to use their large numbers to ram through their route preferences.

The foresight and preparations of the Interstate Trail partisans paid off hugely. Although no route was selected at that very contentious initial meeting, the delegates did decide that Kansas City, St. Joseph, Des Moines, and St. Paul were to be "cardinal points" on the Jefferson Highway route, which, in effect, made the Interstate Trail the front-runner for eventual route selection. Moreover, a threat from a more easterly route running from St. Louis to St. Paul through Iowa cities along the Mississippi River was eliminated, and so was an even greater threat — the so-called Kansas plan, which would have taken the new highway to Omaha and the Dakotas, bypassing Iowa entirely. Lafayette Young's stellar job of keeping the meeting from running out of control very likely also played some part in securing this last outcome.

Most press coverage following the close of the New Orleans meeting attributed the foregoing results to the large turnout and coordinated actions of the Interstate Trail delegates. Several publications even interpreted the meeting's choices of Lafayette Young as permanent chair and E. T. Meredith as JHA president as partisan victories engineered by the supporters of the Interstate Trail. For instance, the *Sioux City Tribune* (as copied in the *Waterloo [Iowa] Evening Courier and Reporter* on November 27, 1915) concluded ruefully that "Des Moines had kidnaped [*sic*] the Jefferson Highway project."

The skillful maneuvering by the partisans of the Interstate Trail was further exhibited at the follow-up meeting of the board of directors, held on February 3, 1916, in Kansas City. The board's most important task at this meeting was determination of the route that would connect the cardinal points specified at the New Orleans meeting. The board members arriving from Iowa and Minnesota gave a strong hint of what route between Kansas City and St. Paul was likely to be favored: somehow, in each of those two states the people chosen to fill the positions of state vice president and the three directors not only were residents of cities or towns located on the Interstate Trail but also were officials in the Interstate Trail Association.

Two of those directors were, of course, W. A. Hopkins and Hugh H. Shepard, who once again ably advanced the case for selection of the Interstate Trail, this time successfully fending off the claims made on behalf of three other routes. Two of these ran between St. Joseph and Des Moines—the Saints Highway and the Ayr Line—and the third was the so-called Chillicothe route, which bypassed St. Joseph in connecting Kansas City and Des Moines. The proponents of the Chillicothe route, defeated at the meeting, tried to keep it alive as a variant of the Jefferson Highway under the name "Blue J Route of the Jefferson Highway," claiming in a route guide issued in 1916 that both it and the Jefferson Highway had been organized at the November 1915 meeting in New Orleans. The JHA was able to stymie the infringement, however, by threatening a lawsuit and protesting to the Iowa State Highway Commission, with whom the Jefferson Highway was officially registered.[7] Forced to back off, the promoters of the Blue J Highway registered it as a separate highway in March 1917.

The Jefferson Highway got even more competition when three other Iowa registered highways—the Daniel Boone Trail, the Mississippi River Scenic Highway, and the Pershing Way—also came into being partly as a consequence of the failure of some towns and cities to entice the Jefferson Highway to come their way. Some towns and cities omitted from the Jefferson Highway's route in Iowa continued to agitate for route changes, and one of those efforts succeeded: in 1921, the highway was extended west from Nevada to Ames, thereby cutting Shipley, Cambridge, and Elkhart from the route. But this route change was a highly defensible one making very good sense, no other major proposals for route alterations in Iowa had anywhere close to the same plausibility or chance of succeeding, and the Jefferson Highway had no difficulty holding its own against competition from other north-south routes across the state.

If threats to the integrity of the Jefferson Highway in Iowa were minimal and easily addressed, during the JHA's entire existence it nonetheless faced very hefty challenges to the highway's official route in some other states. As late as 1925, for instance, even as numbers were about to replace names on highways, Hugh Shepard, then the JHA president, spent his entire year in office contending with major route issues in Kansas, Arkansas, and Louisiana (discussed in chapter 4). However, not many of the JHA's thirty-two state directors and 623 county officers ever had to confront or spend much time on warding off threats to the official Jefferson Highway route. Instead, their energy and attention were taken up by other responsibilities, all neatly summarized in an article, "Anniversary Address," published by W. A. Hopkins, then president of the JHA, in the February 1918 issue of *Jefferson Highway Declaration*.

In his article, Hopkins identified nine categories of duties, the first eight of which dealt with such matters as building goodwill for the highway locally; raising money by subscription for the support of the JHA; keeping pole markings and signage in good order; making sure that the highway was free from obstructions and that needed repairs were made; and seeing to it that the highway was properly graded, drained, and dragged. The ninth category—"to urge the building of a hard surfaced '365-day in the year' road"—was the most demanding one, setting forth an expectation that reached far beyond mere maintenance of the existing highway.

These were big responsibilities to place on unpaid volunteers, but Hopkins pulled no punches: "Each county officer is expected to be very active in the discharge of his duty. If any are not active, they should resign and give place to men in their county who are willing to do the work." Warning that traffic on the Jefferson Highway was already "crowding in upon us," he exhorted his fellow JHA officials to "'Get Busy' in the duties to which they are assigned." The ranks of the JHA must have been filled by many individuals approaching the high level of competence and commitment of W. A. Hopkins, Lafayette Young Sr., and Hugh H. Shepard, because these grassroots agents of the JHA certainly did get busy, and within only another dozen years, the hard-surfaced, 365-day highway that Hopkins called for was a reality.

3 Building the Highway

Even the most enthusiastic devotee of building a hard-surfaced, 365-day automobile highway stretching from Winnipeg to New Orleans must sometimes have been daunted by contemplation of the large scale and complexity of the undertaking. How, exactly, did the JHA's founders think that the ambitious project could be carried out, and what was their plan for meeting its great costs? A brief unsigned editorial, presumably written by editor E. T. Meredith, appearing in the very first issue of *Jefferson Highway Declaration* (February 1916) argued that there was no single course of action to follow regarding costs. It then suggested some of the ways the costs might be met and the work begun.

"In some cases," the editorial supposed, "community road building will be carried on under plans by which farmers and towns-people get together on certain days and everything necessary is donated, including work, use of teams, and necessary gravel. A feast and general good time follows such gatherings." This quaint scenario of community self-help smacked both of neighborly fellowship and celebration and of the once-widespread practice of convening for several days each year all the able-bodied men between the ages of eighteen and forty-five living in a road district in order to "work off" their respective shares of the "road tax." However, experience had shown this to be a wasteful, ineffectual way of caring for roads and also strongly suggested that amateurs, no matter how well meaning and dedicated, were not likely to be up to the task of producing a durable road fit for automobile use.

According to the *Declaration* editorial, "In many townships and counties the work will be done entirely from county funds provided by bond issues," which money would then be used to pay for competent professional road-building services. This was an obviously better option than a citizens' road crew, but only *if* a majority of citizens in those local units of government actually did approve the sale of bonds for this purpose. In some states, including Iowa until 1919, the authority of counties and towns to issue bonds was highly circumscribed, however, and even in states where it could be done, it was likely that some counties—especially heavily rural ones in which the farm vote was large—would refuse to go into debt for the construction of an improved long-distance highway.

Anticipating the likelihood that some cities and counties would balk, the editorial suggested that adopting a 365-Day-Road-Club plan would nudge them toward providing public money for support of the Jefferson Highway. The plan would allegedly work as follows: "Business men of towns or communities are induced to join a good roads club and to pay a monthly sum in dues. Next, the farmers living on a proposed road are approached and asked to pay ordinarily 25 per cent of the cost of the good roads. The funds from the Road Club dues are supposed to provide another 25 per cent. And when this is made up, county tax commissioners are approached and offered a half price road bargain. The tax commissioners are unable to resist a proposition to build roads where the county will be charged but half price." Not known today, however, is the extent to which the 365-Day-Road-Club plan brought the desired results or was even attempted. In any event, the plan's success would have depended on businessmen, farmers, and tax commissioners all doing their parts, but it's easy enough to imagine one or more of these parties not coming through. Farmers would probably have been the weakest link in the chain holding this plan together, but county road officials also might not have welcomed any new claim on very limited road funds in their districts.

Three months later, in the May 1916 issue of the *Declaration*, J. D. Clarkson, newly signed on as JHA general manager, announced a new plan for financing the highway. Still at the center of the plan was an expectation that many counties would pay for the highway work by issuing bonds for that purpose. Where that didn't happen, JHA would raise the needed money by initiating local "subscription lists" to which JHA would make small donations, presumably accompanied by much fanfare. According to Clarkson, "A lot of moral effect is gained by starting a subscription list with a donation of $100 or so from the highway association. As soon as this is done in the communities where interest is lagging, it is certain to follow that other persons will donate to the cause." To get this program going, Clarkson proposed to raise by donations a separate fund of $80,000 to use for pump-priming the subscription lists. However, given that JHA's coffers were usually low, sometimes verging on empty, it seems unlikely that Clarkson ever got such a large sum for this program. It's also hard to believe that JHA's small donations would very often have had the near-magical effects that Clarkson claimed.

All of these plans relied on decisions and actions taken by private citizens or government officials, or both acting together, at the lowest governmental levels—in counties, cities and towns, even townships and tiny local road districts. This extreme reliance on the grass roots simply reflected the reality that roads had long been and still were considered mainly a local responsibility. In its quest to secure the coordinated efforts needed to build a highway running from Winnipeg to New Orleans through seven American states, the JHA was necessarily dependent, at least at the start, on the compliance of hundreds of local governments arrayed along the route. Notice, too, that none of the JHA funding plans indicated any role for federal or state governments. Involvement by both in the building and financing of highways had begun by then, but in the opening days of 1916, it was not yet apparent what large parts each would soon play. In these unpromising circumstances, the JHA's quest for the construction of an interstate highway seemed nonetheless to get off to a very good start. In fact, so impressed was Clarkson by the early results that in May 1916 he proclaimed his conviction that the highway would be completed before the end of 1917.

Although Clarkson's prophecy proved to be wildly off the mark, it wasn't simply a product of what in a later era would be dubbed "irrational exuberance." Clarkson recognized that the highway's route incorporated some mileage that had already been substantially improved—true for portions of the Interstate Trail, for instance. In fact, on the first sociability run, Walter Parker of the New Orleans Association of Commerce had learned from JHA sources that as much as 25 percent of the route already was considered hard-surfaced and that sufficient money was thought to be assured for the hard-surfacing of another 25 percent in the near future. Clarkson was encouraged, too, by the many counties along the entire route that very promptly approved bonds for improvement of the highway. Texas was especially noteworthy in this respect; as reported in the July 1916 *Declaration,* two of the ten counties on the Jefferson Highway's nearly 240 miles in that state had already hard-surfaced the road, and the other eight counties had voted to issue bonds to pay for its hard-surfacing in their jurisdictions. Early *Declaration* issues also brought the good news from Louisiana that, thanks to the approval of bonds in a number of parishes early in 1916, another

200 miles of newly hard-surfaced highway was expected in that state early in 1917.

Many other early occurrences along the route also signaled a widespread strong commitment to the Jefferson Highway. For instance, the *Times Picayune* of New Orleans reported (as copied in *Declaration*, May 1916) that some businessmen in Kansas City had organized a Thousand Club, by which "one thousand men there have each pledged themselves to give $10 a month, $120 a year, to be spent in working up good roads enthusiasm outside of Kansas City," and from the large sum thus raised the Jefferson Highway could certainly expect to be a major beneficiary. Here and there along the route public or private money was also being directed toward grading the road, building culverts, or replacing wooden bridges with concrete ones. Particularly impressive, and covered frequently in *Declaration* articles during that journal's first year, was an agreement reached between Eufaula and McAlester, Oklahoma, to replace a ferry that carried Jefferson Highway travelers across the wide and dangerous Canadian River with a twelve-span concrete bridge projected to cost $150,000. Using Clarkson's subscription-list method, the two cities had raised $75,000 for the project, and the remaining $75,000 needed was provided through sale of bonds. Negotiations were also under way for an early start in building the highway elsewhere in Oklahoma by using convict labor; as reported (*Declaration*, June 1916) by W. F. Dodd, one of that state's JHA directors, this would not only cut costs greatly but speed up the building schedule, inasmuch as "we would otherwise be compelled to vote [to approve bonds] before we could start to build roads."

Contrasting starkly with Oklahoma's use of convict labor, however, was the volunteer labor directed to road building in several places in Missouri, very much in line with the description of community action presented in the JHA editorial. In a hilly section north of St. Joseph, so the Missouri JHA vice president reported at the board of directors meeting in July 1916, an association of farmers "has been constantly at work, cutting every hill without aid, and during six months I should say that little association has delivered not less than a thousand days of labor and have cut and topped every hill in their section." In support of this work, the local JHA chapter donated the money needed to complete the project's construction of concrete culverts. Matching even more closely the editorial's scenario of neighborly cooperation at the local level was the construction in two days of 1.25 miles of road between Carthage and Jasper. Of this charming grassroots event, the *Carthage Democrat* (copied in *Declaration*, November 1916) gave the following crisp account: "Wednesday 86 men worked with 38 teams. They hauled 314 loads of rock and placed [them] on the road. Thursday 52 men were at work with 267 teams and hauled 307 loads of rock. The roadway was built 18 foot wide and the gravel placed 10 inches deep at the crown of the road. The ladies of the Methodist Episcopal Church, South, furnished a free dinner for the laborers."

If encouraging reports like these steered Clarkson to his early conviction that a finished highway was nearly at hand, he must soon have known that was not going to happen by the end of 1917. At their meeting in February 1916, the JHA board of directors had, in fact, adopted a resolution specifying 1919 as the target date for the hard-surfacing of the highway, and following another board meeting in November 1916, President Meredith revived the call for a highway "Hard Surfaced by 1919." That deadline went unmet, however, and any hopes for the highway's completion in the early 1920s were also unfulfilled. As late as January 1926, at the annual JHA meeting, retiring president Hugh Shepard announced that he expected that another three years would be needed to finish the highway's hard-surfacing.

This time the projection was on the mark. In 1929, in its final route guide (issued even after numbers had replaced names on America's interstate highways), the JHA could at last proclaim that the Jefferson Highway was an "all-year route practically all hard-surfaced," which was a true claim so long as "practically all" was accorded a reasonable looseness of meaning. The guide documented the claim by indicating the road surface to be found at every point on the route.

Since the JHA's first days, however, expectations for hard-surfacing had risen, and the new desideratum was a road paved with concrete or asphalt. Although the 1929 route guide identified substantial sections of the Jefferson Highway already paved in all of the states—for instance, the long stretch in Minnesota between Little Falls and Geneva and most of the highway in Missouri and Kansas—it also revealed that much of the highway still was surfaced in gravel. However, because many large-scale paving projects were in progress at that time on the Jefferson Highway in Minnesota, Iowa, Oklahoma, Texas, Arkansas, and Louisiana, in not many more years a hard surface at nearly all places on the Jefferson Highway would have meant a concrete surface. As of the early 1930s, in fact, because so much new paving had been completed in Minnesota, and because the entire highway through Iowa now had a concrete surface, a motorist could already have been assured of a pleasant drive on a mostly concrete-paved road from north-central Minnesota at least as far as Joplin, Missouri, and would have encountered much pavement beyond, no matter which of the two routes was followed to New Orleans.

By any reasonable measure, the replacement within less than two decades of a mostly dirt road by a mostly concrete-paved automobile highway was a great achievement. By the time it happened, however, the highway's name had been replaced by numbers, and JHA was not the main agent bringing the project to fruition. In expecting to wrap up their project quickly, JHA's early leaders clearly had not calculated correctly all of the complications involved in building a 2,300-mile highway. In addition to the multitude of government jurisdictions involved in road building and the uncertain access to the large sums of money needed were such other complicating circumstances as the great variations found along the long route in preexisting road conditions, in terrain and soil characteristics, and in the availability of road-making materials. For faster progress on so large and complex a project, greater coordination of efforts and more money were needed than could be obtained by the efforts of the JHA. When increases in both coordination and money finally did come, moreover, they did so via an emerging federal-state partnership that soon displaced the JHA and all other trail associations as the principal agents in the securing of a national highway system. All of the features of this historic episode are illustrated nicely by the portion of it that took place in Iowa.

Recall that the route of the Interstate Trail taken over by the Jefferson Highway in February 1916 consisted of an original segment (Kansas City to Des Moines) laid out in 1911 and an extended segment (Des Moines to St. Paul) added in 1915. In Iowa, the route entered the state from Missouri a few miles south of Lamoni; ran through three counties (Decatur, Clarke, and Warren) until reaching Des Moines (Polk County); and then moved north through five more counties (Story, Hardin, Franklin, Cerro Gordo, and Worth) before exiting the state into Minnesota a few miles beyond Northwood. This was a very well-marked auto trail when it was absorbed by the Jefferson Highway in 1916, but otherwise how well developed was it? At the July JHA board of directors meeting that year in St. Joseph, E. C. Harlan of Indianola, one of the founders of the Interstate Trail and now a JHA director, reported that the highway was "dirt roads in most of the state." As for condition and accessibility of the road for automobile use, he concluded that "if it don't rain, we have a consistently good road; if it rains, my hands are up; I don't go."

Harlan's account was not up-to-date about the road's surface, however. Six months earlier, Hugh Shepard, general manager of the northern branch of the Interstate Trail, had filed a report with the Interstate Trail Association detailing an extensive amount of graveling of the portion of the Interstate Trail lying north of Des Moines. In that report, excerpted in *Declaration* of February 1916, Shepard noted that the entire length of the highway was graveled in Worth County; all but 2.25 miles were graveled in Cerro Gordo County; in Franklin County, "one-fourth to one-fifth of the road is graveled," and the balance was scheduled for completion by the end of summer in 1915; in Hardin County, one-half of the road was hard-surfaced, including 1 mile of pavement; and in Story County, plans called for graveling the entire length of the highway by the end of 1915. If not accurate in application to the entirety of the highway in Iowa, Harlan's description did fit the highway south of Des Moines, the portion he would have known best as a resident of Clarke County. That segment of the highway, even though its promotion had had a five-year head start on the northern segment, still had no hard surfaces anywhere outside towns and cities. Doubtless, too, it was as impassable in wet weather as Harlan indicated.

This contrast in the extent of development of the Interstate Trail above and below Des Moines was vivid and substantial but not truly perplexing; it followed mainly from the different problems of road building presented in the northern and southern sections of central Iowa. The latter section was located in the Southern Iowa Drift Plain, Iowa's largest geological landform. Because this is the oldest of Iowa's glaciated areas—the glacier retreated about one hundred thousand years ago—it has also been subject longest to erosion. The result is a picturesque landscape carved deeply by rivers and streams and featuring successions of hills that share the height of the original glacial plain but then fall away in rolling descents into deep valleys, soon rising again in equally steep ascents. As noted by geologist Jean C. Prior, this is the familiar Iowa landscape that travelers on Interstate 80 mostly see and that Iowa artist Grant Wood depicted in some of his prints and paintings.[1] But it is a landscape not fully cooperative with Iowa's early preference for building roads running along section lines laid out every mile, north and south, east and west, across Iowa. These characteristics of the terrain through which the Interstate Trail and subsequently the Jefferson Highway coursed in southern Iowa made necessary much grading, filling, and construction of bridges and culverts before any hard-surfacing of the highway there could even be contemplated.

Fewer obstacles stood in the way of building the highway north of Des Moines. There the highway followed a route through a completely different Iowa landform, the Des Moines Lobe, which was produced by a much later glacier. Because this glacier receded from Iowa only ten thousand to twelve thousand years ago, erosion has not had as much opportunity to alter the leveled landscape left behind in the wake of its retreat. Here are found far fewer of the hills, valleys, and streams seen in the southern part of the state, and the much smaller presence of those landscape features greatly reduced the amount of preparatory work needed in construction of the highway north of Des Moines. Also facilitating the building there was the plentiful presence of gravel, a resource in short supply along the route south of Des Moines.

These differences made road building easier, and its per-mile cost much lower, in the highway's northern counties. This was a matter of considerable consequence in an era in which the construction and upkeep of roads, as well as the obligation to pay for them, were matters left, for the most part, in the hands of counties and townships. Under these circumstances, the respective paces of improvement in the roads of the counties were bound to vary considerably. Even in instances in which road upkeep was pursued diligently, needed but costly major improvements were likely to be slow in coming when funding had to be pieced together through combinations of property taxes, special assessments for roads, "workings off" of the road tax, donated money and materials, and, after 1911, county allotments from the state's automobile registration fees. (Not until 1919 did counties have the authority to raise money for road projects by issuing bonds.)

Mostly on their own in paying for roads, counties also had complete control over the quality of work done on culverts, bridges, rail crossings, and the surfacing, grading, draining, and dragging of roads within their jurisdictions and could determine the routes of roads as well as which ones should have priority for maintenance and upgrading. A greatly improved road might abruptly meet up with an unimproved continuing road at the county line; indeed, there was no certainty that there would even be a road there of any kind with which it could connect and con-

Figure 10. Thomas H. MacDonald, Iowa State Highway Commission chief engineer, ca. 1919. Photo courtesy of Iowa DOT. © Copyright Iowa Department of Transportation. All rights reserved.

tinue. These were not the best of circumstances for creating a network of decent state roads, let alone for building roads that aspired, like the Jefferson Highway, to span many states.

A modest encroachment on the original extreme decentralization of road authority in Iowa came in 1913, when the state legislature gave a reorganized state highway commission the power to supervise the engineering aspects of the road work done by county and township officials, even though the latter continued to have full authority to initiate and carry out projects. To direct the commission's supervisory responsibilities, the new law also created the office of chief engineer, to which Thomas H. MacDonald, a young civil engineer on the commission's meager staff, was appointed (figure 10). MacDonald's appointment proved to be a fateful one, for both Iowa and the nation.

His engineer's sensibility offended by the unscientific, inefficient, and wasteful road-building practices surviving in Iowa from the nineteenth century, MacDonald set out to achieve roads built to engineering standards suitable for the twentieth century. Because the highway commission lacked the powers to initiate and direct road projects, under MacDonald's leadership much of its early effort was directed toward activities falling under the broad headings of research and public education. Able at least to block questionable projects, the commission used that power as a basis for achieving sound road-building results through close consultation with county officials. This practice fit nicely with MacDonald's belief that, because the traffic on virtually all roads is overwhelmingly local—that is, local users going short distances in the vicinity—roads should be designed and located to accommodate the needs of those users. For MacDonald, it was an obvious corollary of this view that a long-distance highway—for instance, the Jefferson— could not be a separate undertaking simply imposed on the landscape by engineers and planners from on high but rather should be a composite of connected roads meeting local needs in the first instance.

State involvement in local road projects in Iowa grew modestly again following passage of the Federal Road Act of 1916, the first major federal legislation supporting road construction to be enacted since the early nineteenth century. Providing $75 million over a five-year period for grants for rural roads, with amounts to be matched equally by the states, this act directed that the money was to be administered by the state highway commissions, which were charged to maintain quality control over the projects on which the money was spent.

Accepting the 50 percent matching obligation and other terms of this law in 1917, the Iowa legislature also directed the state highway commission to determine on which roads the federal aid could be spent. This directive was placed in the Iowa law at the prompting of MacDonald, who wanted to avoid having the federal aid frittered away on roads that went nowhere in particular or failed to hook up with the roads of adjoining counties. Since becoming chief engineer in 1913, he had consulted with county officials to create a system of interconnected main roads in Iowa. Initially believing that from 10 to 15 percent of Iowa's roads would make up this system, he finally concluded that the range would be 5 to 7 percent.

From the new law's directive came the highway commission's designation in 1919 of two systems of roads in Iowa: a primary system of about 6,400 miles of roads that connected every town and city having at least one thousand residents—about 6 percent of Iowa's roads—and a secondary system of 10,000 miles of county roads and 87,000 miles of township roads. Because the Jefferson Highway easily qualified as a primary road in Iowa, any projects connected with it were eligible to receive federal funds. However, the highway commission still lacked the power to initiate those or any other projects or to direct funds to them. The commission did have to approve construction plans for roads in the primary system, and it also controlled the release of money from the primary road fund; nonetheless, all projects were still proposed by county officials, who also remained in charge of carrying out the work.

The first big move made toward the eventual upending of Iowa's lingering fondness for local control over primary roads followed the enactment of the Federal Aid Highway Act of 1921. Continuing the requirement that a state match a grant by an equal amount, this law provided much greater funding than was authorized in the 1916 act but also specified that the money could be spent only for road work *determined by, and under the direct control of,* the state highway commission rather than county officials; no longer would a single county be able to disrupt development of a statewide or interstate highway by failing to take action to improve its roads. Moreover, unlike the 1916 act, the 1921 act restricted expenditures to roads that were part of a state's primary road system. The roads included in that system, which could not exceed 7 percent of a state's total road mileage, would ultimately be approved by the federal Bureau of Public Roads, but only after consultations with the highway commission in that state. Those consultations began with the state highway commission recommending the roads a state believed should be included. The goal was to achieve an interstate system of improved automobile roads in the United States built on consensus and cooperation between the state and federal governments and paid for by financial support provided by both.

If major features of the new federal law seem unusually reminiscent of the convictions and practices that MacDonald developed in Iowa (which historian Earl Swift has nicely summed up as his "collaborative, bottoms-up approach"), the reason is that those convictions and practices powerfully shaped the 1921 law.[2] Having acquired an enviable professional reputation as chief engineer in Iowa, MacDonald was the obvious choice for appointment as director of the federal Bureau of Public Roads when that position opened in 1919, and after pushing his views for two years in Washington, he had considerable support in Congress. Prior to his federal appointment, MacDonald had also been a prominent figure in the American Association of State Highway Officials (AASHO), which endorsed his views on a federal-aid highway system for the United States and incorporated them in a bill submitted to Congress. That bill became the law enacted in 1921, which Earl Swift has convincingly described as "the single most important piece of legislation in the creation of a national [highway] network," the foundation for the system of numbered highways emerging in the late 1920s as well as for the system of limited-access interstate highways built after World War II.[3] This law not only increased the authority and involvement of both state and federal governments in road building but also began a very durable state-federal partnership. Because MacDonald stayed on as bureau chief until 1953, he was able to foster that partnership for more than three decades, and today it is still in place, in all essentials standing as designed by its principal architect.

MacDonald had favored creating a highway system through a state-federal partnership partly for financial reasons: even if Congress charged the federal government to construct a system of national highways, he felt certain Congress would never—could never, as a matter of political realism—appropriate the immense sums needed for that purpose. By enlisting the states in the road-building activity on a fifty-fifty matching basis, the federal government could cut its financial obligation in half. From the states' point of view, this would surely be perceived as an excellent arrangement, because it increased the money in hand needed to carry out one of their traditional responsibilities, and it did so at the very moment when the fast-growing ranks of automobile owners were making an even faster-rising clamor for better roads.

In spite of the seemingly very good deal provided by the 1921 federal law, however, the Iowa legislature was in no hurry to accept its terms, especially its required transfer of responsibility for maintenance of primary roads and control over their surfacing from counties to the state highway commission. The legislature's approval of all conditions came at last in 1925 in a state law that, in addition to authorizing more money for the primary road fund through a two-cent per gallon gasoline tax, created, within the primary road fund, a subaccount called the "primary road development fund." It was this special account that would receive and match equally all federal funds and be under the complete control of the state highway commission. The remainder of the primary road fund would continue to be spent at the discretion of the counties, subject only to technical and engineering review by the highway commission. Also, as in the past, distribution of this money to the counties would be based on their geographical sizes, a method that had long been justifiably denounced as being both inequitable and irrational. If these were still not ideal conditions for the swiftest completion of

Figure 11. Fred White, MacDonald's successor as chief engineer of the Iowa State Highway Commission, ca. 1919. Photo courtesy of Iowa DOT. © Copyright Iowa Department of Transportation. All rights reserved.

the hard-surfacing of Iowa's primary road system, however, at least the highway commission now had more than its foot within the door; for the first time it actually had access to a large sum of money subject only to the commission's determination of how and where to use it on behalf of the state's primary roads. In the latter half of the 1920s, the increments to that special development fund, derived from equal federal and state shares, were a bit more than $4 million annually.

When MacDonald resigned as chief engineer of the Iowa State Highway Commission in 1919, Fred White, his assistant, moved up to fill that position and continued the practices and policies begun under his predecessor (figure 11). Held back by limits on the state highway commission's authority and on the funds under its control, neither MacDonald nor White was ever in a great rush to pave roads. Instead, both patiently and systematically pushed for a high-quality level of completion of all the necessary work preparatory to paving—grading, draining, building concrete culverts and bridges, eliminating dangerous railroad crossings, shortening routes. But how would the commission use the money over which it now had significant control?

When a reporter for the *Des Moines Tribune-News*, C. C. Clifton, posed that question during a visit to commission headquarters in May 1925, he learned that there were no definite plans yet. However, "the three commissioners and the chief engineer [Fred White] said flatly they are not going to use [the development fund] to pave stretches of road." Instead, "county boards would be invited to co-operate" on projects on which funding support from the highway commission would supplement funds provided by counties. When Clifton characterized this as "helping the county which had helped itself," the commissioners and chief engineer White replied that "they were going to do exactly that— help those counties which help themselves."[4]

In his article, Clifton noted two ways in which counties might act to "help themselves": they could commit their annual receipts from the primary road fund to projects that the highway commission was also ready to support, or they could raise their share of the needed funds for such jointly desired projects by issuing bonds. As matters turned out, the latter method made all the difference for completion of the Jefferson Highway in Iowa, bringing that big project to a close by the end of the decade.

In 1919, the Iowa state legislature had extended to counties the power to issue bonds to raise money for paving roads and also authorized them to use annual receipts from the primary road fund to pay down the principal amounts of their borrowings. Until 1927, only twenty-five of Iowa's ninety-nine counties had ever voted to obtain road funds in this way, and of this group, Cerro Gordo and Polk were the only counties through which the Jefferson Highway passed that had used this option to pay for paving their portions of the highway. A sudden big rush to pass county road bonds came in 1927 following the state legislature's passage of a law raising the amounts counties could borrow and authorizing them to use their shares of primary road funds to pay down both principal and interest on their bonds. In that year alone thirty-one more counties committed to borrowing money for paving their primary roads, including five more Jefferson Highway counties: Worth and Franklin, both in the northern half of the Jefferson's route in Iowa, and all three of the counties—Warren, Clarke, and Decatur— located in the more rugged terrain through which the highway passed below Des Moines.

By 1928, the highway commission, following its policy of helping counties that help themselves, had paving projects on the Jefferson

Highway under way in all five of these counties, and thanks to Mac-Donald and White, almost all the foundational work of grading, filling, draining, and bridging was already done, so this paving was completed by 1929. This left only the portions of the highway in Story and Hardin Counties in central Iowa in need of a paved surface. Harboring much rural opposition to going into debt to pay for paved roads, both counties had voted down road bond proposals several times, most recently in 1927, even as so many other counties were approving bond issues. Facing ever greater pressure to join in completing the paving of the Jefferson Highway (a large segment of that highway also overlapped the Lincoln Highway, now known as US 30, in Story County), both counties finally approved bond issues in the spring of 1929. Soon paving of their portions was under way, and due to the excellent preparatory work on the road, the paving job was completed in the summer of 1930.[5]

So there it was at last—a completely paved highway crossing Iowa from the Minnesota to the Missouri border. Indeed, because Minnesota had also just completed paving its portion of the highway as far north as Wadena and, except for the first 2 miles below the Iowa border, much paving had also been done in Missouri, there was now a 600-mile stretch of mostly paved highway reaching from the North Woods of Minnesota almost to Kansas City. Since 1926, there no longer was—officially, at least—a Jefferson Highway but instead only a highway bearing numbers, lots of them in Minnesota, but in Iowa, just two—US 65 from the state's northern border to Leon and US 69 from there to the state's southern border. Whether referred to by the new numbers or the old name, however, the highway was clearly the fulfillment in Iowa of the dreams of the promoters of the Jefferson Highway and, before them, of the Interstate Trail. Among the most excited and emotionally engaged witnesses to this great moment was Hugh Shepard, who was determined that the historic event would not slip by without receiving due recognition and celebration.

To commemorate the event, Shepard at first proposed building a permanent archway over the highway at the Minnesota-Iowa border, but the state highway commission nixed that as an obstruction. Shepard then proposed placing a monument at the side of the highway. That plan went through, and with much fanfare at a celebration held in the fall of 1930 and attended by the governors of Iowa and Minnesota, a concrete monolith was installed next to the highway at the shared border of the two states (figure 12). The words "Iowa" and "Minnesota" were incised on the monolith's south and north sides, respectively, and a bronze tablet facing the highway carried this inscription: "This marker, dedicated October 28, 1930, by Governor Theodore Christianson of Minnesota and Governor John Hammill of Iowa, commemorates the completion of The Jefferson Highway across their states."[6]

That blustery October day saw a joyful celebration marking the great event, one of master organizer Hugh Shepard's biggest and most eye-catching productions. The reporter filing the account of it in the October 30 edition of the *Northwood Anchor* estimated that over five hundred automobiles, coming in large caravans from both Minnesota and Iowa, brought approximately two thousand guests to the event. As the official in charge of the proceedings, Shepard introduced the two governors, who each gave a speech remarking on the significance of the occasion and, armed with scissors, jointly cut a red, white, and blue ribbon straddling the highway. The Northwood High School band treated the celebrants to a musical program featuring the "Iowa Corn Song," "Hail, Minnesota!" "America," and "God Save the King" (the last in recognition of the Jefferson Highway's terminus in Canada). After the ceremony, two hundred of the throng departed for Mason City to attend a banquet hosted by that city's Commercial Club at the Hotel Hanford. Master of ceremonies for the continuing celebration was, of course, Hugh Shepard.

Although the JHA was nearly an extinct organization by that time, its last president, George McIninch of St. Joseph, Missouri, was at the festivities, bringing with him official greetings from the governor of his state. Sad to say, however, several of the people most directly involved in the building of the Jefferson Highway in Iowa and Minnesota could not attend. A contract letting on the day of the celebration prevented Fred White from being there. Thomas MacDonald had been in Iowa only days before the celebration leading a tour of visiting foreign highway engineers, but because he had to take the entourage next to Detroit, he couldn't stay for the event. Another major participant in the highway's completion had been Charles Babcock, Fred White's counterpart in the Minnesota highway commission. Although he had done much to push along the development of the highway in that state, the US State Department had asked him to take over the task of hosting the visiting foreign engineers in Detroit, so he, too, had to miss the celebration.

Figure 12. Erected at the Iowa/Minnesota border in 1930, this monolith commemorates the paving of the Jefferson Highway in those states. Photo by Mike Kelly.

Figure 13. On October 28, 1930, W. A. Hopkins (*second from right*) and colleagues set a speed record on the fully paved Jefferson Highway in Iowa. Photo source not known. From author's collection.

However, one major figure from the earliest days of the Jefferson Highway was there—W. A. Hopkins, founder of the Interstate Trail Association in 1911 and former president of the JHA. No one—not even Hugh Shepard—had a longer-standing connection to the highway than Hopkins, and on this happy occasion he was eager to make a point. Leaving the Missouri state line just below his hometown of Lamoni at 6:00 a.m., he, his driver, and two passengers in his Chrysler 8 reached the Minnesota state line above Northwood at 9:51 a.m. (figure 13). They had covered 244 miles in 231 minutes (rest-stop times included), averaging 1 mile every fifty-six seconds, or a bit over 63 miles per hour, a rate of speed not even permitted on that stretch of highway today. No one could miss or gainsay Hopkins's point: following two decades of effort by him and other promoters of the Interstate Trail and the Jefferson Highway, a new day of motoring on that route at last was at hand.

4 ||| Marking the Highway

It was already clear by 1925 that the Jefferson Highway would be fully paved within the near future. Every state through which the highway passed had made it a part of that state's primary road system, thereby putting the highway high on each state's list for improvement and making it eligible in each state for the expenditure of federal matching funds; assisted by these favoring circumstances, paving was well under way and would continue to make rapid progress. Far less certain, however, was the continuing status of the highway. Two questions loomed: How much longer would there be a highway identified as the Jefferson Highway? What role, if any, lay ahead for the JHA?

What pushed these questions to the fore was the prospect of interstate highways being assigned numbers in place of the names bestowed on them by the trail associations. In truth, many of those named highways already were numbered over lengthy stretches, thanks to their running through states that assigned numbers to their primary roads. One such state was Iowa, in which the Jefferson Highway after July 1920 was also posted by the state highway commission as Iowa Primary Road No. 1. In November 1924 a committee of the AASHO recommended the development and implementation of a plan by which numbers and specifications for signage would be applied in a coordinated manner to all interstate highways.

Adopted by AASHO, the recommendation was forwarded to the US secretary of agriculture, in whose department the Bureau of Public Roads was lodged. The secretary then established a Joint Board on Interstate Highways consisting of representatives of both state highway officials and the Bureau of Public Roads to look into the matter and make proposals for action by AASHO. The secretary's choice to chair the joint board was the bureau's chief, Thomas H. MacDonald, who once again was situated at the center of critical decision making affecting the main features of the American highway system. Chairman MacDonald strove, as usual, to secure consensus among the state highway departments, on whom the full implementation of a final highway plan would rest. The joint board met in Washington, D.C., in April and August 1925 and also held six regional meetings in May and June of that year, finally producing a report in late October 1925. Following another full year spent considering proposed changes submitted by state highway commissions, the joint board sent a final report to the secretary of agriculture, who approved and forwarded it to AASHO. That organization adopted the report in November 1926 and called on the state highway commissions to implement it.

As it happened, the person within the JHA first having to grapple with the likelihood that changed circumstances lay just ahead for the Jefferson Highway and the association was Hugh Shepard, who was JHA president in 1925. His presidential correspondence throughout that year reveals an acute awareness that important changes were imminent and that the uncertainties about the future of the highway and the JHA were much on his mind.[1]

Within two weeks of taking office, Shepard sent a letter (January 12, 1925) to Fred White, chief engineer of the Iowa State Highway Commission, reporting that at its forthcoming annual meeting the JHA would be "taking stock to determine whether the Jefferson Highway really fills a community need or whether the need of a separate organization is over" for any purpose other than "perhaps to retain the franchise and preserve the name of the organization." What prompted this inquiry, he explained to White in a January 15 follow-up letter, was Shepard's understanding that, in a likely new system of federal highways, "the Jefferson Highway in its entirety from New Orleans to Winnipeg will be taken over by the various State Highway Commissions and its markings will be retained and kept up by the Highway Commission[s]." In both letters he solicited the Iowa chief engineer's opinion about the continuing need for the JHA in these circumstances. Because White had also served as president of AASHO during the preceding two years, his advice would presumably have special authority.

In his reply (January 16, 1925), White first pointed out that Shepard had a "wrong impression" of what AASHO proposed to do, which was not to take over and continue the marking of the highways with names but rather to replace names with numbers. Under the proposed new system, he claimed, the Jefferson Highway would carry one number for its entire length, and the signs indicating that number would be posted and maintained by state highway commissions. Any marking of the road with Jefferson Highway signs, he added, "would have to be [done] through the efforts of the Jefferson Highway Association as at present." Because he thought that would be a worthwhile ongoing activity for the JHA, White recommended continuation of the association, which he believed had already done "an immense amount of good for the development of our highways."

White's understanding of the new highway identification system then under development appears to have been as wobbly as Shepard's, however. The routes of some named highways—for instance, the Jefferson Highway and the Lincoln Highway—very likely would be incorporated close to their entireties into the new highway system, but everyone involved in the design of that new system agreed that no route should be assigned a single number. To do so would be to grant it a kind of continuing separate recognition and, more important, to ignore the need to subordinate all decisions about numbering to the requirements of a rationalized national highway system.

The hundreds of privately sponsored named highways, taken together, came nowhere close to being that coherent national highway system; moreover, because portions of trails very frequently overlapped, motorists all too often faced a bewildering profusion of trail signs on the road. Far from wishing to accommodate the trail associations, then, the AASHO members pushing for highway reform were determined to move past the motley agglomeration of named highways and to do more than merely accommodate their continuation with numbers in place of names. That applied to the Jefferson Highway no less than to any other named highway. In spite of White's assertion to the contrary, the route of the Jefferson Highway would not carry a single number, as Shepard was to learn by the midpoint of his year as JHA president.

But what about White's notion that the JHA could continue to put up its distinctive signs, even as the state highway departments also mounted signs bearing the route's new numbers? And what about White's specific encouragement of the continuing existence and activities of the JHA? White's advice on the former question failed to present AASHO's position fully and accurately, and on the second question, his blithe assurance did not convey AASHO members' true feelings about the continuing presence and role of the trail associations.

As historian Earl Swift has observed, by the mid-1920s "the trail associations, helpful though they'd often been in automobiling's early days, had become unnecessary, time-consuming, and meddlesome third parties in road-building decisions."[2] AASHO's call in 1924 for a coordinated system of numbered highways rested in part on a widespread wish among highway officials to be done with the trail associations. If names were the problem for which numbers were judged to be a large part of the solution, didn't it follow that the trail associations should be directed to cease all ongoing signage activities and take down all of their existing signs? If that were done, of course, the demise of the trail associations would quickly follow.

Mandating such action was not something that AASHO could do, however, nor could it be done by the secretary of agriculture, the Joint Board on Interstate Highways, or the Bureau of Public Roads. Because the roads constituting the new system of numbered highways were perceived as "owned" by the respective states and completely under their control, the success of that new system depended on its voluntary acceptance by all the states and their voluntary compliance with its terms. Moreover, from the start of its deliberations, according to a letter dated April 13, 1926, from Chairman MacDonald to Senator Earle Mayfield of Texas, members of the joint board accepted "that the naming of highways was a matter entirely within the jurisdiction of the States, and if individual States desired to perpetuate the [trail] names there would be no interference on the part of the Joint Board, nor would any action by the Joint Board prohibit the continuance of those names." MacDonald added that "it was informally agreed by the members of the Board that should the States desire to carry the names of the highways on the same standards carrying the numbers adopted for the interstate highways as recommended by the Board, that the Board would make no objection."

If neither the joint board nor AASHO could mandate, nothing prevented the latter from making recommendations to its members, which it did by adopting Resolution No. 5, "Regarding Trail Marking," at its annual meeting in November 1924. Distinguishing in the resolution between "reputable trail associations" and those that were merely fraudulent money-squeezing schemes, AASHO warned citizens to be wary of the latter and then resolved "that this Association hereby recommends to the several States that the reputable trail associations now existing be permitted to continue their markings during their period of usefulness, pending the establishing of the proposed marking system, unless such action shall conflict with the marking system and policies now in force in the several States." The resolution also recommended "that no trail association be permitted to establish further routes on State or Federal-Aid routes."

Resolution 5 is loaded with ambiguous phrases—"reputable trail associations" (which were they?), "their period of usefulness" (how determined?), "pending the establishing" (wasn't that likely to happen soon?)—that hinted strongly at AASHO's wish to narrow the reach, number, and continued existence of the trail associations. At the same time, the resolution made clear that no more trail associations were welcome and that state highway departments should not let existing trail associations get in the way of implementing signage programs. Affirmed here, too, was the principle that states were in charge of all matters having to do with roads.

It was this last point that White had neglected to take into account when assuring Shepard that the Jefferson Highway trail signs could continue to go up. Accommodation of a trail association's signs in one state might not be matched by accommodation in another state, and if that were to happen, continuous and full markings of a trail association's highway would be impossible. Shepard learned that truth during his term as JHA president.

Why did White fall so far short of giving good counsel to Shepard? After all, he was AASHO's president when Resolution 5 and the resolution calling for a new highway system were adopted; freshly retired, he should have been fully informed about the features of each, as well as of the many controversies that would likely follow in their wake. Indeed, following AASHO's approval of its subcommittee's call for an overhaul of the nation's highways, White had presciently observed that "as soon as the purpose and work of the proposed board shall become known, the infernal regions will begin popping."[3] But the JHA stood high among the "reputable trail associations" referred to in Resolution 5, the Iowa State Highway Commission had always had a cordial and productive working relationship with JHA's Iowa contingent, and in Iowa the JHA could continue to post trail signs. Perhaps White was simply lulled into generalizing from his experience in Iowa and concluding that the forthcoming new highway system would present no challenge to the existing high regard for the Jefferson Highway and its promotional association. But perhaps, too, he had simply let an unusually large dollop of Iowa politeness shape his reply to fellow Iowan Shepard.

Buoyed by White's encouraging but off-base counsel, Shepard concluded not only that the JHA should press on with trail markings but it should be the association's highest-priority activity during his year in office; indeed, he aimed to have the highway completely marked by the end of his term. He reasoned that, if that task could be out of the way by the time the states had put up their official signs and had finished paving the highway, the JHA could thereafter focus solely on publicizing the highway.

Shepard had set for himself a very big job. Even though the JHA was now ten years old, portions of the original trail were still not adequately marked, and some—perhaps many—earlier trail markings doubtless needed repainting or replacement. There were also some relocated routes (in Kansas, for instance) and new route additions (for instance, across Arkansas and from Winnipeg to Winnipeg Lake, and Denison to Dallas to Shreveport) that needed to be marked. Of course, a full-scale effort to complete the trail markings as quickly as Shepard desired would have imposed on the JHA a large immediate expenditure of time and money, inasmuch as good trail guidance required many stenciled signs with varied content (figure 14). That demanding scenario was averted, however, by Shepard's instant entanglement in organizational problems that took up an inordinate amount of his time and attention and stymied his efforts to raise the amounts of money needed for trail marking. Soon Shepard's initial presidential bullishness about the prospects of the Jefferson Highway during 1925 began to falter, and in an April 23 letter to a Kansas JHA official, he confessed that "I am somewhat discouraged over the Jefferson Highway outlook."

At the bottom of Shepard's distress was frustration deriving from JHA's inability to secure the funds needed to do the trail markings—or to do much of anything else, for that matter. State chapters were assigned dollar quotas determined by rules adopted by the JHA, and one of the duties of state officers was to make sure those dollars were received for support of JHA's activities. During Shepard's term in 1925, however, even the most supportive states fell far short of meeting their full quotas, and from some states no money came in at all. Shepard's letters frequently contained laments about JHA's poor financial condition; in a July 18 letter to a JHA operative in Kansas, for instance, he confessed that "just now, we are living a hand-to-mouth existance [*sic*]." That situation never improved during his tenure as president.

Part of the fund-raising problem doubtless stemmed from the rising uncertainty about the continued existence of the Jefferson Highway in the new system AASHO was proposing, but perhaps some of the problem came from the fact that in 1925 JHA was then ten years old and within sight of achievement of its goal of a fully paved highway. In

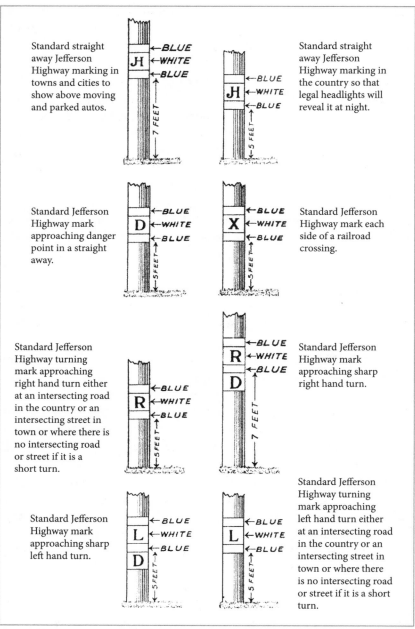

Figure 14. Some of the stenciled trail markings that JHA used to communicate important information to drivers. Adapted from the *Modern Highway*, November 1920.

several letters, Shepard noted ruefully that he couldn't get JHA officials in some locations (for instance, Joplin, Missouri) even to reply to his letters, let alone meet financial commitments. In places where the highway was already paved and marked, the need for making continuing contributions must have seemed less urgent than in earlier years, especially since the funds would now be put to use for trail markings only and no longer for the more compelling goal of securing the hard-surfacing of the highway. The association had also by early 1923 ceased to publish a monthly magazine, which had once played a large role in maintaining the fervor of members and reinforcing the view that they were all working together to secure a highway, all of whose sections were equally essential to the success of the whole.[4]

Adding to the fund-raising problem (and providing further evidence that member solidarity had begun to soften) were some route disputes with which Shepard had to grapple during his entire term. After its first several years, the JHA had been relatively free from having to deal with major route problems, but now came big, contentious disputes in three states—Kansas, Arkansas, and Louisiana.

In truth, all of the route disputes followed from JHA's own actions. The one in Kansas, for instance, resulted from JHA's effort (ultimately successful) to adopt a more direct route between Kansas City and Fort Scott, thereby trimming the distance by about 30 miles. Defenders of the original, longer route secured the support of the state's secretary of state, a cagey politician who, in a long and amusing epistolary sparring with Shepard, kept finding ways to deny the frustrated JHA president's requests for information and public records. In the case of Arkansas, the dispute accompanied that state's admission in 1924 to full membership in JHA and consequent entitlement to having a trunk route run through the state.[5] There had been an official "scenic" branch route in the western part of the state from the start, but there also were many supporters within the state for placing the newly designated trunk highway on a central route running through Little Rock and then on to Alexandria, Louisiana. Some even favored a route that would take the highway southeastward from Little Rock and across the Mississippi River before turning due south, thus bypassing Louisiana altogether until nearing New Orleans. Throwing his support behind the central route, the newly hired JHA general manager, A. J. Keith, convinced the JHA advisory board that it should be recognized as the official trunk route.

Keith and the other JHA officials, including Shepard, quickly learned that a central route through Arkansas would affect the continuing route in Louisiana in a way not acceptable to JHA members in Louisiana. An October 30, 1925, letter from a Louisiana state JHA official to all JHA parish leaders in Louisiana put the matter bluntly: "As you are aware, we have practically withdrawn from the Association, and have so advised its officials, on account of being ignored regarding the Arkansas cut-off. . . . It is our opinion that Louisiana should take no further interest in the Jefferson Highway Association until her wishes that the marks through central Arkansas be removed and the western Arkansas from Joplin to Shreveport marks are respected." Lest the letter's main thrust be missed, the writer reaffirmed that Louisiana "will take no further part in the organization unless any JH marks now on the Central [Arkansas] route are removed." Thereafter, no funds for the JHA treasury were forthcoming from Louisiana, dues collections from Kansas for the entire year were piddling, and contributions from Arkansas fell far below Shepard's expectations, as he lamented in several letters. Route controversies, he learned the hard way, tended to shrivel the enthusiasm of outraged members and disinclined them to make donations.

For the sour turn of events in Louisiana, Shepard seemed to hold general manager Keith principally responsible; in a letter dated November 9, 1925, he lamented that Keith "has estranged us wholly from the state of Louisiana." If that unpleasant outcome was Keith's doing, it presumably had some connection to his active and successful pushing for adoption of the central Arkansas route that so alienated the Louisianans. In fairness to Keith, however, it should be noted that the central Arkansas route already had plenty of local support—so much, in fact, that, early in Shepard's term, in an April 23, 1925, letter (the same one in which he reported being "somewhat discouraged") Shepard wrote that "it begins to look as if we might have to go through Eureka Springs, Harrison and Russellville [and thence on to Little Rock] in order to get the active support [locally] that we need."

Although JHA did end up adopting that central route, it later reversed its decision, and its last route guide, issued in 1929, showed the western, formerly scenic branch route, also identified there as US 71, as the official Arkansas trunk route. The Louisianans, it appears, had succeeded in overturning the original determination to run the highway through central Arkansas and had secured instead their preferred route. The exact succession of events leading to JHA's reversal remains to be determined, but evidence that much controversy and confusion must have prevailed in the interim could be found in the 1926 edition of *Clason's Touring Atlas of the United States*. There, the Arkansas map showed the Jefferson Highway running along the central Arkansas route and then dropping south (actually, more like south-south-*west*!) to Alexandria, Louisiana, whereas the Louisiana map had the Jefferson Highway coming to Alexandria via the old scenic route from Shreveport.

Over the course of Shepard's year in office, his exasperation with Keith grew steadily. This must have been especially galling for the president, inasmuch as it was he who, at the start of his term, had "found" Keith and recommended that he be hired for the open position, as he acknowledged in the November 9 letter. (Previously Keith had been a publicist for an insurance company and a stellar salesman for the Burroughs Adding Machine Company.) In earlier letters Shepard had professed satisfaction with Keith's promotional work, especially in Oklahoma, Texas, and Arkansas, but by midyear his letters began to carry complaints that Keith had developed a proclivity for being on the road for long intervals completely out of touch with both the JHA home office and the JHA president and, even worse, that the general manager's efforts were not bringing in the money needed to support JHA's activities.

His confidence in Keith at last fully depleted, Shepard raised a question with his advisory board in September 1925 about Keith's continuing value to JHA and proposed on October 12 that the general manager be fired. Keith, he acknowledged, had done good work in making contact with the "right kind of people" in Oklahoma, Texas, and Arkansas, toward the ends of building good organizations in those states and publicizing the JHA and the highway there, but his salary and expenses had begun to exceed the amounts raised by his efforts. "Mr. Keith," Shepard summed up, "has the ability to drive the nail but not to clinch it," adding later in the letter that "Mr. Keith is not a detail man, and does not give detailed reports of his activities and the money does not seem to be coming in, so I am of the opinion that it is best for the Jefferson Highway Association to continue its activities with the cooperation of the State Vice President and Directors in each state, and to dispense with the services of the General Manager." The advisory board didn't concur, however, believing that Keith's work would eventually bring good results. Rebuffed, Shepard then went to work on persuading Keith to resign, and by the end of the year he had succeeded and the general manager was gone.

In his November 9 letter, Shepard had also observed that "Mr. Keith has not succeeded in collecting money enough in the last two months to pay his salary and expenses while at the same time I have collected between $2000 and $3000 from northern points [that is, Manitoba, Minnesota, and Iowa], doing this by correspondence and personal contact at a cost of $25 a month to the Jefferson Highway Association." Convinced by his easy success in fund-raising that there was much more money to be tapped along the route, Shepard proposed that state JHA officials be urged to go after it and that most of the money be dedicated to trail marking. Of the amount he had personally raised, $1,600 came from donors in Winnipeg, St. Paul, and several places in Iowa in response to Shepard's appeal for money to be spent on trail markings in Oklahoma and Texas. For this purpose, he had contracted with a sign company to begin putting up stenciled pole marks on November 1.

In order to proceed along this line, Shepard wanted the full concurrence of his advisory committee, and once again, he couldn't get it. Serving on that committee was a former JHA president, Arthur Shafer of Pittsburg, Kansas, whose endorsement Shepard particularly wanted. However, Shafer refused to support Shepard's proposal, arguing that the money should go first to reimburse the expenses already incurred by him and other JHA directors and officers in attending several of their recent meetings. Here, perhaps, was further evidence of a general falling off of members' enthusiasm and commitment from JHA's earliest days: not all JHA officials were as ready as Shepard to keep on donating personal funds and unreimbursed time on behalf of the cause, especially as that investment of time also cut into attention to their business interests (in fact, even Shepard in his letters had begun to join Shafer in lamenting this personal cost). In any case, the advisory committee's opposition made clear that its members didn't share Shepard's sense of urgency about getting the marking of the highway done in 1925. To the end of his term, Shepard was still struggling to win the advisory committee's support for this activity, as numerous exchanges of letters with Shafer reveal. In one of those letters, dated December 19, the embattled JHA president acknowledged that "I am sure I will be greatly relieved when my term of office expires next month," perhaps a sentiment also held by some members of his advisory committee.

Poor Hugh Shepard! Probably no one else had ever come to the JHA presidency determined to do so much and prepared to invest so heavily of personal time and fortune, only to face so many obstacles and to accomplish so little of what he set out to do. As the end of his term approached, his big sign-painting project was still not under way (and whether it was ever carried out remains unknown but seems unlikely). Not only had his determination to put the association on a more business-like basis been swamped by staffing problems and the difficulty of raising funds, but he had to devote an inordinate amount of time to route controversies and membership schisms. It was Shepard's misfortune to take office at a time in which JHA's earlier successes likely had brought many JHA members to a point of weakening commitment. Their lessening of attachment probably was also helped along by the uncertain policy environment confronting JHA following AASHO's proposed changes in the nation's highway system.

Shepard had already gotten a strong hint as early as May 27 that his other big concern—that the Jefferson Highway be incorporated as a whole and under a single number into that new system—was problematic, when he attended the joint board's regional meeting in Kansas City. On July 24, Shepard followed up with a letter to E. W. James, secretary of the joint board, asking whether Shepard and others from all the Jefferson Highway states could come to Washington, D.C., "to properly present the claims of the Jefferson Highway for selection as a national highway." In his July 29 reply, James unfurled a masterpiece of evasion: "The Board will not hold hearings and feels that it has all information necessary for carrying on its work. . . . Since my talk with several representatives of your Association at Kansas City I am very certain you will feel that the Joint Board has handled the whole situation regarding the named trails fairly and considerately in view of the actual conditions which must be met." Could anyone receive a reply like that and not know that the cause was lost?

When the joint board's preliminary plan was released in October 1925, probably the only surprise for Shepard was just how far the plan departed from his hoped-for adoption of a single number to cover the entire route of the Jefferson Highway, and this unwelcome outcome was retained in the final version of the plan adopted by AASHO in November 1926. The many segments of numbered highways that soon replaced the Jefferson Highway through the various states were as follows:

Minnesota—US 75, US 2, US 71, US 10N, US 10, US 65
Iowa—US 65, US 69
Missouri—US 69, State 4, US 71, US 66
Kansas—US 73E (now US 69), US 66
Oklahoma—US 66, US 73 (now US 69), US 75
Texas—US 75, US 80
Arkansas—US 71 (for western route), US 65 (for central route)
Louisiana—US 71, US 61, US 90

In sum, segments of no fewer than thirteen numbered highways—several ending in one state only to reappear in a more distant, noncontiguous state—had abruptly displaced the Jefferson Highway. In these results were major implications for the content of road maps and the signage motorists would now encounter in driving the old route and—even more important for Shepard—the prospects for the continued recognition of the Jefferson Highway.

Shepard's unhappiness with these unfolding events was shared by many others. A brief unsigned piece published in the *New York Times* on June 18, 1927, for instance, lamented that the highways were now "sprinkled . . . with signs that bear cold numerals instead of names that glow in American history." The article reprinted approvingly a colorful snippet from an article first appearing in the Lexington (Kentucky) *Herald*: "The traveler may shed tears as he drives down the shady vista of the Lincoln Highway or dream dreams as he speeds over a sunlit path on the Jefferson Highway. . . . But how in the world can a man get a kick out of 46 or 55 or 33 or 21?" The newly assigned numbers also inspired a sarcastic reaction by Henry Joy, president of the LHA, who suggested that the great transcontinental highway could now be formally described as "the Lincoln Highway, a memorial to the martyred Lincoln, now known by the grace of God and the authority of the Government of the United States as Federal Route 1, Federal Route 30, Federal Route 30N, Federal Route 30S, Federal Route 530, Federal Route 40 and Federal Route 50."[6]

The regime of highway numbers had great utility, however, and, in any case, it was here to stay. Whatever lingering feelings of bitterness or disappointment Shepard may have had, by 1928 he was ready to put a positive spin on recent developments in the highway system and to praise the contribution of the JHA to those developments, now emphasizing the JHA's role as a pathfinder for and developer of a major component of the new system. As he proudly noted in a speech delivered in 1928, "The work of the Jefferson Highway planners was so well done and the highway so carefully selected that the Jefferson Highway for practically its entire distance was placed on numbered United States highways forming a part of the main trunk line system of highways in the United States."[7] He also found great satisfaction in JHA's part in promoting paving of the highway, as evidenced by his joyful, even ecstatic, participation in the celebratory event at the Minnesota-Iowa border in October 1930, as recounted in the previous chapter, and in another event the year before celebrating paving the highway between Des Moines and the Missouri border, briefly noted in chapter 7.

But what role was left for the JHA? Or was there any longer a need for it? First posed by Shepard in his letter to Fred White at the start of his term in 1925, these questions were all the more relevant in the new era of numbered highways. However, the organization continued through the rest of the decade. At a meeting in April 1929, the JHA advisory committee, still pondering the future of the organization, decided to once again recommend keeping it going, and a month later, the JHA headquarters, still located in St. Joseph, announced that twenty thousand Jefferson Highway maps were ready for free distribution. Accompanying the announcement was a somewhat wistful statement from JHA president George McIninch: "Despite the present day system of numbering roads, sentimental and historical significance attaches to the name of the Jefferson Highway. It is the aim of our association, through publication of maps and by many other organized efforts, to retain the identity and prestige of the Jefferson Highway." The 1929 map was the last one issued by JHA, and what those "many other organized efforts" may have been, if any, remains unknown. President McIninch did show up for the event in October 1930 that celebrated the completion of paving the highway's route in Iowa and much of Minnesota, but ready evidence of any further significant activity by JHA is virtually nonexistent, and presumably the organization, whether by formal dissolution or mere withering away, was soon gone.

Already well aware by 1928 that an era was nearing an end, delegates to the annual meeting of the JHA in that year had passed a resolution conveying their hopes "that the importance of pioneer transcontinental highways like the Lincoln Highway and the Jefferson Highway shall be nationally appreciated and that the location and memory of these highways shall be perpetuated to posterity."[8] Their pride in their work and their wish for its lasting recognition were well justified, but within only several more years the likelihood of their hopes being realized had fallen precipitously. What realistic prospect could there be for anchoring the Jefferson Highway in the collective memory in the absence of distinctive trail signs posted along the highway, or of a name affixed to a route on road maps, or of an organization dedicated to publishing route guides and otherwise publicizing the Jefferson Highway?

A strong hint of just how quickly all recollection of the Jefferson Highway was likely to fade came as early as 1934. In June of that year forty delegates from twelve cities along US 65 met in Des Moines to incorporate the US Highway No. 65 Association for the purpose of resisting a perceived loss of traffic on US 65 to other north-south highways through the Midwest. According to an article in the *Mason City Globe-Gazette* (June 30, 1934), "Tribute was paid at the meeting to the pioneer Jefferson Highway. . . . It was pointed out, however, that the Jefferson had broken up into various other highway associations . . . and that all highway organization of the day is along the line of publicizing these federally numbered highways." Further, the article noted, although "a move to attach the word 'Jefferson' to the name met with some early favor," others were concerned "that claiming it might offend some of those whose support would be needed for organization and extension." (This may have been an allusion to possible fallout from the earlier route controversy in Louisiana, inasmuch as US 65 followed the route in central Arkansas and Louisiana that had so provoked the ire of the Jefferson Highway organization in the latter state.)

But another stated reason for rejecting continued appropriation of Jefferson's name must truly have stung the name's advocates: "It was pointed out that a new generation had come up since this name was best advertised." In other words, after seven years' experience of driving on numbered highways, the opponents believed that most drivers were not likely to make any meaningful connection between the numbers on those highways and the old names, including even such revered ones as Lincoln and Jefferson. In these circumstances, the Jefferson Highway and the impressive work done on its behalf by Hugh Shepard and his many colleagues in the JHA were destined to pass very quickly from the general recollection into the near oblivion in which they have remained ever since.

The Jefferson Highway and its early advocates deserve better than that, however. The highway's promoters helped bring into existence a major highway, and that highway is still there, even though disguised in its final incarnation by a multitude of numbers. The most direct way now to recognize their work and to grasp the magnitude of their achievement is to get out on their highway and follow it from "Pine to Palm," looking for the highway's features, remnants of the highway's impact on the roadside, the widely varying landforms with which it had to cope, and the changing landscapes through which it passed. To provide a start in that searching out of the old named highway still lurking behind the numbers, the next three chapters trace the highway's original route in Iowa, noting major variants of the original highway and its successor highways in the state—US 65 and US 69—as well as some features of the roadside that have survived from an earlier time. The route laid out in these chapters can also be traced in a Google map available at the JHA website (www.jeffersonhighway.org; click on "Maps" and then "Iowa").

Presentation in the following three chapters reflects the reality of three distinctive phases of the highway as it descended from north to south through Iowa. Chapter 5 traces the highway for 109 miles from the Minnesota-Iowa border to the small town of Colo in central Iowa, following the road into many small towns and through much flat, highly productive farmland and noting some outstanding roadside structures surviving from an earlier era. Chapter 6 covers a 45-mile segment of the highway between Colo and Des Moines, bringing into view an early major route relocation, some important improvements in the early highway, and a thwarted attempt at highway redesign by the Iowa State Highway Commission. Chapter 7 completes the survey of the highway, taking it for nearly 90 miles from Des Moines to the Missouri border. That phase of the trip goes through rugged terrain utterly unlike that of north-central Iowa and presented problems to road builders unlike any they ever had to face in the northern segment of the highway in Iowa. For further help in placing these three segments of the old highway and the towns, cities, and counties through which they ran, readers should consult an Iowa road map.

5 Looking for the Highway
Minnesota Border to Colo

After November 1926 motorists intending to follow the Jefferson Highway (same as Iowa Primary Road No. 1) in Iowa would have found that the route from the Minnesota-Iowa border to Leon, Iowa, was now marked US 65, and from Leon into Missouri, it was US 69. Nearly ninety years later, those two numbered highways still make up the same north-south journey across the state, but the proportionate contribution of each has changed. Today's motorists making that journey take US 65 to Des Moines, where that highway now merges with US 69. They then stay on US 69 once the two highways have parted a few miles south of Indianola and follow that highway to the Iowa-Missouri border.

Those nine decades have also brought changes to the exact route indicated by those two highway numbers. Most have been relatively small changes involving such things as straightening the route and bypassing towns (although there has been much less of the latter than on some other major highways in Iowa, such as US 30). True, one change was a big one: since 1938, US 65 no longer reaches Nevada and Ames and instead runs south from Colo until moving southwest toward Des Moines. The highway today also follows a bypass route at Des Moines that skirts the eastern edge of the city. In spite of these changes, the route of the Jefferson Highway, at least as it was when its paving was nearing completion in the late 1920s, can be followed much of the way today on US 65 and US 69. A traveler looking for the route of the Jefferson across Iowa will therefore often be on those two highways.

Frequently, however, that traveler will not be on US 65 and US 69, because the Jefferson that was assigned numbers in 1926 and then paved with concrete by 1930 had already departed in many places from the Jefferson's route as originally laid out and refined in the highway's earliest years. Pursuing the Jefferson Highway in its earliest state in Iowa therefore also entails some traveling on back roads, especially between the Minnesota border and Des Moines. Although most of these roads were, at the highway's inception, little more than dirt paths, today virtually all are paved or graveled county roads. In at least one place, however, a short segment of the Jefferson's earliest dirt-surfaced route remains—as it happens, at the very point of entrance of the original Jefferson Highway route from Minnesota into Iowa's Worth County.

WORTH COUNTY

To find this relic and begin the search for the Jefferson Highway across Iowa, start on US 65 at the Minnesota-Iowa border, the site of the 1930 monolith celebrating completion of the highway's paving, and from there go south 0.5 mile to the first cross road (505th Street). Take this gravel road west for 0.1 mile until reaching the intersection with another gravel road, Mockingbird Avenue. Stop here and look north; the two-track dirt lane in view is a remnant of the route of the original highway (figure 15). Eleven feet wide, this road, now a private one used for access to the adjacent farm field, runs for about four hundred yards until dead-ending at a point where the original road would have crossed the railroad tracks there. Avoiding that rail crossing may have been one reason that the route slightly to the east, now US 65, was finally chosen for the Jefferson Highway. The latter route to Northwood had the additional merit of being a bit shorter and a whole lot straighter than the original route.

To trace the stair-stepping original route from this point into Northwood, the first Iowa town on the highway, travel south 0.7 mile on Mockingbird Avenue to 495th Street, where gravel ends and pavement begins. Continue another 0.5 mile until reaching 490th Street. Turn east here and go 0.6 mile to Nightingale Avenue, at which point turn south and go about 1 mile to 480th Street. Turning east at this intersection, follow 480th Street for about 0.5 mile until reaching US 65, and then turn south and follow that highway (which also is Eighth Street N.) until reaching Central Avenue in Northwood.

Central Avenue is Northwood's main commercial street, which retains much economic vitality today, doubtless helped considerably by the fact that Northwood (population of 1,264 in 1910 and 1,989 in 2010) is the county seat. In the four commercial blocks on Central Avenue that constitute a historic district listed in the National Register of Historic Places are many buildings that were there in the era of the Jefferson Highway. Included, too, on that historic district's southern edge is a public park along the Shell Rock River that once provided a free tourist

Figure 15. Looking north at a dirt-road remnant of Jefferson Highway entering Iowa north of Northwood. Photo by Mike Kelly.

camp to travelers on the Jefferson Highway. A 1923 JHA campground guide identified this facility as an "eleven acre camp [offering] electric lights, water, rest house, shade, free fuel, tables, and benches." The guidebook also noted that Northwood's amenities included "a modern three story hotel" and "a half dozen modern garages." Those early garages have long been gone, but the hotel referred to—known then as the Winifred but subsequently as the Northwood—continued operations for over one hundred years until closing in December 2014. A simple brick building, today it lacks some original decorative railings but otherwise is not much changed in appearance from its earliest years (figure 16). To reach the Hotel Northwood, just pull ahead across Central Avenue and go one very short block on Eighth Street S. to the intersection with First Avenue S.

The opening of the Winifred in 1913 was a major event in Northwood, prompting the editor of the *Worth County Index* to proclaim (May 8, 1913) the new hotel to be "the greatest material benefit which has come to Northwood in many a long year." In recent decades, however, the hotel did not so much cater to travelers as provide, in the words of an April 20, 2003, *Des Moines Register* article, a "safe haven" and a "shelter from the world" for most of its residents, who also tended to

Figure 16. Originally named Hotel Winifred, the Northwood Hotel in Northwood welcomed travelers from the earliest days of the Jefferson Highway. Photo by Scott Berka.

"become family." The expectation in Northwood is that the hotel building will now undergo some remodeling and be reopened, perhaps offering both apartments and rooms for transients. If so, Hotel Northwood will resume its part as a rare surviving direct link to the earliest days of motoring on the Jefferson Highway.

To follow the route of the Jefferson (same as US 65) through Northwood, return to Central Avenue, go east for two blocks, and turn south on Tenth Street S. On the southwest corner of the turn is Worth County's second courthouse, now housing the county historical society. Across the street diagonally is the county's third and present courthouse. Completed in 1893, it is a handsome building but much more modest in size and ornamentation than the usual Iowa county courthouse. As described in its National Register statement, it is "an extremely simplified version of the Victorian Romanesque, perhaps indicating a small construction budget."

Continue south on US 65, noting on the northeast corner of the intersection with First Avenue S. the remains of the Watts service station, long closed but built in 1928 and therefore almost of the vintage of

Figure 17. In Kensett, looking east on Fifth Street, the town's main business street and route of the Jefferson Highway. Photo by Scott Berka.

those "half dozen modern garages" touted in the early highway guides. Not many blocks ahead at the south edge of Northwood, look for the Royal Motel, a longtime fixture on US 65, on the west side of the highway. Opened in 1953, this eight-unit motel has been impeccably maintained and is now in the care of its fifth owners and operators, Daniel and Debra Luedtke. The Luedtkes also own and manage two other mid-1950s vintage motels on US 65, in Albert Lea, Minnesota, and Manly, Iowa. In its earliest days, the Royal Motel had a neon sign and a miniature golf course, both now long gone; otherwise, the motel today looks much as it did at its opening, and the replacement backlit sign is a beauty, displaying the motel name and a regal crown atop the motto "Fit for a King."

The next 6 miles of US 65 going south coincide exactly with the route of the Jefferson Highway and lead to the small town of Kensett. In town, US 65 becomes Maple Street, but at Sixth Street the present highway parts ways with the old Jefferson route. To follow the latter, at Sixth Street turn east off Maple Street, travel one block to Elm Street, and then proceed south one block to Fifth Street. Turn east on Fifth Street onto what has always been Kensett's main business street (figure 17).

In the nineteenth century, having lost the contest with Northwood to be the county seat, Kensett continued to be a very small town. The twentieth century brought no change in that respect. In 1910, Kensett still had only 360 residents, and now there are even fewer—only 266, according to the 2010 census. No surprise, then, that little commercial activity remains on Fifth Street. Perhaps, too, the rerouting of US 65 away from Fifth Street in the late 1920s was another factor initiating a long-term toll on that street's economic vigor.

Kensett was once a lively presence on the Jefferson Highway, however. One of its prominent businesses was the Jefferson Highway Garage, a Ford dealership located at Sixth and Elm Streets, where the fire station now stands. The town also maintained a public tourist camp, described in the 1923 guide book as having "capacity 100 cars, electric lights, water, comfort stations, abundant shade, free fuel, tables and benches." During the sociability run in the fall of 1916, Kensett took the prize (a tank-car load of road oil) for having the greatest number of automobiles (272) in proportion to town population.

Resuming the tour of the old highway, travel two blocks east on Fifth Street to Main Street, which, counter to the usual expectations raised by that name, is and always has been a residential street, not a commercial one. Follow Main Street south for 0.4 mile to the town's edge, at which point the street name changes to Orange Avenue and a patch of 1.9 miles of gravel begins. Stay on Orange Avenue to 400th Street, turn east and go 0.2 mile, then south on Partridge Avenue. At 390th Street, pavement resumes. Travel another 2.3 miles into Manly. There Partridge Avenue becomes Broadway Avenue, which carries the Jefferson Highway all the way through the town.

Manly's inclusion on the Jefferson Highway was not the only big news coming out of that town in the second decade of the twentieth century. In 1912, the Chicago, Rock Island and Pacific Railroad had settled on Manly to be one of that company's major hubs, and the consequences of that decision were profound, as detailed in a special January 7, 1915, edition of the *Manly Chief.* Suddenly construction was under way of a magnificent new terminal, a round house having twenty stalls, transfer-shed trackage for 640 freight cars, various railroad shops, and a power plant. Soon sixteen passenger trains came through Manly every day. Because the town was also a three-way division point for the railroad, all passenger and freight trains coming through Manly changed crews there. In consequence, a great influx of railroad workers and their families quickly followed, adding more numbers to the many construction workers there temporarily. As the newspaper account noted, Manly suddenly was "famous as the fastest growing town in Iowa."

The 1900 census had put Manly's population at 359, and ten years later it had even fallen off a bit to 346 residents. By 1920, however, even

Figure 18. In Manly, the Jefferson Highway ran along the west side of the former Manly Hotel. Photo by Scott Berka.

after the temporary surge in population attributable to construction work had ended, the town's population had made an enormous (427%) jump to 1,476. The count in every subsequent census has remained within relatively close range of that number, although the eventual decline in railroad operations in Manly, culminating in the liquidation of the Rock Island line in 1980, has been matched by a slight long-term decline in Manly's population, which in 2010 stood at 1,323.

As a consequence of its unusual circumstances of growth, Manly soon had more hotels than the usual small town could boast in the early twentieth century—at least three, and one of them happened to be located on Broadway Avenue at Elmore Street (one block south of Main Street), making it well positioned to cater not just to transient railroad workers and passengers but also to growing numbers of travelers on the Jefferson Highway. Built in 1895, it was known initially as the Doebel Hotel, but by sometime in the early 1920s the name had been changed to the Manly Hotel (figure 18).

Although the hotel long ago ceased operations and has not been put to any other uses for many years, the old building—red brick, two stories, flat roof—still stands at that location, albeit in a state of advanced decrepitude. For most of its life, the hotel consisted of twelve rooms (all sharing one bathroom!) on the second floor and, on the first floor, a lobby, office, large kitchen, dining room, living quarters for the owners, and an open porch. Sometime in the early 1930s a tavern, accessed by an outside stairway, was added in the basement. By the end of that decade, however, the tavern and the dining room had closed, after which the space may have been converted into more rooms; at the time of the hotel's sale in 1946, a newspaper story claimed the hotel then had thirty rooms. When the Manly Hotel ceased operations is uncertain, but it probably was used for an indefinite period thereafter as an apartment house. The front porch and the outside stairway to the basement have been closed off for many years.

Memories of the Manly Hotel's connection to the Jefferson Highway linger on in Manly. According to local lore, for instance, John Dillinger and some of his gang and their "molls" stayed at the Manly Hotel the night of March 12, 1934, prior to robbing the First National Bank in Mason City the next day. The details of the alleged encounter at the Manly Hotel provided at the time by its then-owner seem quite solid and convincing. However, "Dillinger stayed here!" (or plug in the name of any other notorious mobster of the 1930s) was once a well-known highway legend attached to many tourist camps and small-town hotels throughout the Midwest in that decade. Sometimes, of course, the claim was true, but in this instance apparently some uncertainty remains. According to an article published online by the *Mason City Globe-Gazette* on January 9, 2014, Terry Harrison, a Mason City Public Library archivist, has concluded that the Dillinger gang actually came down from the Twin Cities on the day of the robbery in Mason City.

In 2007 Manly used a grant received from the Iowa Community Visioning Program to develop a plan for the restoration and preservation of the Jefferson Highway corridor through Manly, and some of the decorative parts of that plan have since been carried out. In 2010 work began on the Manly Junction Railroad Museum, located at 101 E. Main Street, whose doors opened in 2015. Dedicated to documenting and celebrating the railroading past of the town once known as Manly Junction, this museum is the loving creation of two brothers, Dan and Mark Sabin, and their nephew, Brad Sabin, all of whose efforts were also supported by several grants received from Worth County. The Sabins are descendants of Art Sabin, once a resident of Manly and an engineer for the Rock Island Railroad; now, as owners and officers of the Iowa Northern Railroad, a short line connecting Cedar Rapids and Manly, the Sabins carry on the family connection to railroading. They plan eventually to relocate the museum to a larger, permanent building yet to be built on the north side of Manly.

As local awareness and celebration of Manly's rich history as both a highway town and a railroad town grow, one can hope that the Manly

Hotel—a major surviving artifact connected to both aspects of that history—will eventually come within the scope of the interpretive and preservation efforts already under way in the town. Meanwhile, the historically significant old building hangs on precariously and continues to molder.

The next stop on the route of the Jefferson Highway is Mason City, about 9 miles ahead. To get there, leave Manly by going south on Broadway Avenue, but while doing so, notice the small brick building on the east side in the first block past the Manly Hotel. Today occupied by the Federal Auto Upholstery firm, it clearly dates from the era of the Jefferson Highway and was obviously built to house an auto-related business, probably a service garage.

CERRO GORDO COUNTY

Continue south on Broadway Avenue until the road once again becomes Partridge Avenue. At 340th Street, go east for about 0.5 mile and then turn south on Pheasant Avenue, a gravel road. Now having entered Cerro Gordo County, travel another 3 miles to 310th Street. Turn west, cross the railroad tracks, and at Owl Avenue, notice the sign on the left for "Freeman Preserve." The earliest route guide for the Jefferson Highway identified a Freeman Station located here, but perhaps it was never much more than a rural railroad stop, and the entry disappeared from later route guides. Although the name Freeman Preserve clearly makes a historical reference, all that is covered by it today is a neighborhood of post–World War II residences fronting a private road.

While here, take a close look at the enclosing roadside. From Northwood to this point, the landscape seen from the road has been flat, open Iowa farmland reaching off in all directions into an unobstructed horizon. Here, however, the road is tightly enclosed on each side by a thick wall of trees adjacent to the road. This is a continuously smooth, hard-surfaced drive today, but at least one patch of this verdant country lane was infamous in the earliest years of its incorporation into the Jefferson Highway. As reported in the June 22, 1915, *Mason City Globe-Gazette*, "Mason City automobile owners are making a good many complaints about the condition of a place in the Manly road" where "a farmer named Smith living near Freeman has 'cleaned up' about $250 this spring, pulling automobiles out of this mud hole." Although the article doesn't say so, the farmer may have regularly watered the hole to assure both the gripping consistency of the mud and the steadiness of his income flow. Stories of farmers doing this in the earliest days of motoring abounded—another well-worked category of highway legend, but doubtless the stories sometimes, maybe often, were true.

After traveling west on 310th Street for another 0.5 mile, rejoin US 65 and go south for about 2.5 miles until reaching the northern edge of Mason City and the start of Federal Avenue. About 1.5 of those miles coming up to Federal Avenue are a divided multilane road that bypasses the original Jefferson Highway route, which today can't be fully followed but in part is traced by Nature Center Road. Federal Avenue, the Jefferson's route in Mason City, used to be a straight shot through the city, but in 1985 it was closed off for several blocks to accommodate placement of the downtown Southbridge Mall. Thus, after moving south on Federal Avenue for about 1.5 miles, travelers on US 65 are briefly shunted west one block onto Washington Avenue (and northbound travelers through Mason City are guided east one block from Federal Avenue onto Delaware Avenue). Until reaching Washington Avenue, note the many old commercial buildings still lining Federal Avenue, some quite beautiful.

Follow Washington Avenue for several blocks to Central Park, on the way passing at Third Street NW the Cerro Gordo County Courthouse, a former office building built in 1936 and remodeled for courthouse use in 1960. Central Park is a wooded one-block urban park also bounded by First Street NW on the north side, State Street to the south, and Federal Avenue on the east. Recognizing that the Jefferson Highway would bring many travelers via Federal Avenue into the heart of Mason City, that great booster of both the highway and the city, Hugh Shepard, spearheaded a campaign in 1917 to build a "comfort station" in the park. Whether or not that valuable amenity was ever built, a public restroom facility does stand on the northeast corner of the park today. On First Street NW facing Central Park is City Hall, housed in a modern structure, and on State Street across the park stands the Park Inn Hotel. The latter is a dazzling remnant from Jefferson Highway days.

Although the local chamber of commerce touted Mason City as "the Metropolis of Northern Iowa," the city's population was only 11,230 in 1910 (as of 2010, it had advanced to 28,079). As the county seat, however, Mason City had obvious governmental significance, and served by no fewer than five rail lines, it definitely was also a major regional industrial and mercantile center, as documented in the narrative accompanying its central commercial district's listing in the National Register of Historic Places. Here, for instance, were located a beet sugar factory, a very large clay drainage tile manufacturing plant, and two cement-producing plants (both of which figured substantially in the eventual paving of major roads in Iowa). For a short while, Mason City was the site of the Colby Motor Company, an automobile-manufacturing firm. Further indicating the importance of automobiles to the commercial life of Mason City were the nineteen automobile dealerships located there as of 1920.

In addition to the Jefferson Highway and several lesser roads, the Atlantic-Yellowstone-Pacific (AYP) Highway, an early east-west highway, ran through Mason City. By the very early 1920s, the city had built and maintained a free public tourist camp at the city's East Park along State Street E., which was also the route of the AYP in its approach to Mason City from the east. Known after 1926 as US 18, this highway then departed the city on its west side on Fourth Street S. and headed for the resort town of Clear Lake, the self-styled "Saratoga of the West," 10 miles away.

As of 1918, those 10 miles to Clear Lake were paved with concrete—the first paving project in Iowa to have received federal and state aid, resulting in the first paved intercity road in the state (figure 19). The Iowa State Highway Commission was elated, observing in its September–October 1918 *Service Bulletin* that "while the completion of a ten-mile surfaced highway in some other states would pass without more than a casual mention, yet in Iowa the completion of this ten mile stretch is an epoch marking event." The same article noted that the cement, sand, gravel, and most of the labor used in the project were "Cerro Gordo products," making this "almost entirely a home-made road."

Not just the highway commission but the locals, too, were enthusiastic about the paved road. About five thousand of them showed up for its official dedication ceremonies, which began with speeches and music at the county courthouse in Mason City, continued with an automobile parade that stopped briefly at the halfway point for more speeches and symbolical observances, and ended in Clear Lake with a barbecue dinner served in the city park. As described in the *Service Bulletin*, it was a blowout occasion: "For this dinner there had been prepared three large beeves, roasted in a pit in the park; 1,129 loaves of bread and 6,900

Figure 19. Iowa's first (1918) concrete-paved intercity highway met the Jefferson Highway in Mason City. Postcard by Kruxo. Author's collection.

pickles. Some idea of the crowd and its appetite can be gained when it is known that more than 4,000 huge sandwiches made from the beef and bread, disappeared long before the entire crowd had been supplied." The celebration ended with presentation of a musical program and more speeches in the Clear Lake park.

Although the paved road from Mason City to Clear Lake was not part of the Jefferson Highway, the JHA had no qualms about claiming it in its route guides as a connected "spur" route. Nearly a century later, the road continues as US 18 Business Route, but no indication remains there of its once famous standing in Iowa highway history.

During the nearly ninety years since US 65 officially replaced the Jefferson Highway in Mason City, most evidence of that city's once close ties to the early auto trail has also been eroded. At least two major highway artifacts, both hotels, do remain, however, and amazingly, one of them—the Park Inn Hotel, located at the corner of Federal Avenue and State Street across from Central Park—even evokes today an accurate sense of what the hotel was like when it once welcomed travelers on the Jefferson Highway.

One of six hotels designed by famed architect Frank Lloyd Wright, and the only one still standing, the Park Inn Hotel is a spectacular ex-

Figure 20. Park Inn Hotel, designed by Frank Lloyd Wright, was the original location of the JHA tourist information headquarters in Mason City. Photo by Scott Berka.

ample of Prairie School architecture, exhibiting such tell-tale features as low-pitched hipped roof, far-extended overhanging eaves, and horizontal decorative features in the facade, including rows of casement windows, as well as other aspects of design and decor particularly indicative of Wright's work (figure 20). Although the hotel and its restaurant fill all the building's space today, Wright designed the building complex to also accommodate the City National Bank and a law firm's offices, both of which shared space with the hotel at the opening in 1910. In 1916, the JHA designated the Park Inn as its local "tourist headquarters," and doubtless it was a service well kept up by the JHA's energetic local representative, Hugh Shepard. Here Jefferson Highway motorists not only could get useful travel information but also presumably were often enticed to stay in the hotel or to eat at its restaurant. Certainly the hotel was an aesthetically inviting place, its public spaces and forty-three guest rooms suffused with Arts and Crafts styling and furnishings.

Wright's building had gone up during boom times in Mason City, but its original occupants began to be buffeted by changing economic circumstances in the early 1920s. A severe national postwar economic depression in 1920 was followed by a longer-lasting downturn in Iowa's farm economy throughout the 1920s, and by the middle of that decade the City National Bank had declared bankruptcy. As of 1922, the Park

Inn began to face very strong competition from a much larger and more commodious hotel that opened in Mason City in that year.

Decades of varied uses, alterations, and deferrals of maintenance then followed, during which time the Park Inn property declined alarmingly. Even though placed on the National Register of Historic Places in 1972, as the turn of the twenty-first century neared, the property stood derelict and abandoned, a strong candidate for demolition. In 1999, however, a group of local citizens created a nonprofit organization, Wright on the Park, to which the city sold the property. Then began a campaign to raise funds, restore the property—done at a total cost of about $18 million—and reopen as the Historic Park Inn in 2011.

Where the City National Bank once filled out the complex's east end, there now is a ballroom, and the space formerly taken up by forty-three small guest rooms and shared bathrooms is now given over to twenty-seven larger, more comfortable guest rooms, each having a private bathroom. Within the hotel's altered space, however, all interior furnishings and appointments, such as art-glass panels, wall light fixtures, carpets, furniture, and ubiquitous mahogany trim, are faithful to Wright's intentions, and the hotel lobby and the building's exterior have been meticulously restored to their original appearance. The restoration has secured a remarkable result: a visitor to the hotel today sees substantially what a Jefferson Highway motorist would have seen long ago as he or she turned off Federal Avenue at State Street, parked somewhere near Central Park, and then approached and entered the Park Inn.

Mason City's other significant remnant from Jefferson Highway days is the former Hotel Hanford, located several blocks farther north on Federal Avenue (although the building's front entrance faces Third Street NW). The Hanford was the hotel that, following its opening in 1922, soon ended the Park Inn's claim to be the JHA's local outpost and favored hostelry. An eight-story structure costing nearly $1 million to build, the new hotel offered 250 rooms, each of which, unlike those in the Park Inn, had a private bathroom. The JHA was jubilant that the Hanford had prevailed over another hotel option under consideration at that time after the local advocates of a new hotel concluded that it should be located "on the Jefferson Highway." But all Mason City boosters could revel in the conviction that theirs would soon be hailed as "the big small city with the New York hotel," as it was identified in an article in the November 1922 issue of the *Modern Highway*.

Forty years later, on June 19, 1962, Hotel Hanford was the site of a champagne supper celebrating the opening of the movie version of *The Music Man*, a Broadway musical composed and written by Mason City native son Meredith Willson. As the *Mason City Globe-Gazette* reported the next day, all of the movie's principal actors, as well as Willson, joined many of the city's residents at the Hanford for the gala event that ran deep into the night. Yet by the end of that decade, the city's premier hotel was closed. Sold in 1969 to Good Shepherd, Inc., the Hanford is now the Manor, an apartment building for senior residents. Anyone driving by the massive and beautiful structure today will nonetheless find it looking just as it did in the 1920s, when Federal Avenue brought Jefferson Highway travelers to its doors. (While here, go one block farther west on Second Street NW to the Suzie Q Cafe—not a survivor from the Jefferson Highway era but nonetheless a seventy-year-old Valentine diner still worth the attention of the fan of roadside commercial architecture.)

Mason City has some other impressive sites, most within easy walking distance of the Park Inn Hotel, that any traveler searching out the Jefferson Highway route should be sure to visit while in the city. Foremost on the list of sites not to be missed are the Stockman House, a residence designed by Frank Lloyd Wright; many other Prairie School houses designed by associates of Wright that make up the Rock Glen/Rock Crest National Register district; and next door to the Stockman House the Architectural Interpretive Center, a source of information on Mason City's large holdings of Prairie School structures. Also of interest are Meredith Willson's boyhood home and Music Man Square, which commemorates Willson's great Iowa-based musical. Information about all of these sites, including directions for visiting them on foot, can be obtained from the Visitors Information Office located at Washington Avenue and First Street SW or at that office's website. Not yet on the list of local sites proudly touted by Mason City boosters, however, is another must-see attraction, the Rancho Deluxe Z Garden, located at 500 Second Street NE, several blocks east of the former Hotel Hanford. Assembled from a wide array of cast-off items, such as old bicycles, a bathtub, bowling balls, and commercial signs, many then hoisted high onto walls made of concrete blocks, this zany place is a delightful example of a recognized category of "outsider" art known as "visionary folk art environments."

To continue the journey on the Jefferson Highway in Iowa, go back to the west side of Central Park and resume traveling south on US 65 (it runs on Washington Avenue here, but within several blocks, the path of US 65 out of Mason City shifts to Federal Avenue, along which are strewn a few abandoned gas stations and other highway-related structures from an earlier era). After traveling about 10 miles, turn east on 170th Street, go 0.5 mile to Pheasant Avenue, and turn south. After another mile comes Rockwell, a small town of 700 residents in 1910 (but up to 1,039 as of 2010), which was the last town in Cerro Gordo County on the Jefferson Highway route—but just barely on the route, inasmuch as the old highway fell short of reaching the town's commercial center, instead staying on its western edge. Within only another several miles south of Rockwell, the Jefferson Highway then moved back onto the route followed by US 65 today.

Even this modest accommodation of Rockwell, however, was irksome to those motorists who wanted to move more expeditiously on the highway. An opinion piece appearing in the *Mason City Globe-Gazette* on November 17, 1928, gave vent to the economic aspect of their concern. "I wonder," wrote its unnamed author, "if the average person understands what is involved when a primary road follows anything but the shortest line between two points. Consider the case of the bend in the Jefferson Highway made for the purpose of including Rockwell on the paving. The distance from Hampton [county seat of Franklin County, the next county south of Cerro Gordo County] to Mason City is more than a mile greater than if the road were straightened out." Claiming a traffic count of two thousand cars a day on this portion of the highway, and positing that the average cost of motoring was ten cents per mile, the writer concluded that "this extra mile is costing in the neighborhood of $100 a day for 365 days in the year." Those sharing the writer's annoyance with this deflection from a straight path for the Jefferson Highway and, later, US 65 at last got relief in 1931 when the state highway commission finished paving the section of US 65 that came to be known locally as the "Rockwell cutoff."

Keep moving south on Pheasant Avenue, observing in passing the beautiful Rock of Ages park constructed in the front yard of a house on the west side of the street—another "visionary folk art environment," but this one inspired by religious faith. Then, near the south edge of town, note the abandoned gas station on the east side of the street

Figure 21. A driveway once brought Jefferson Highway motorists under the canopy of this former early gas station in Rockwell. Photo by Scott Berka.

(figure 21). Essentially a small brick house, it has a hipped, overhanging roof and a canopy supported by two brick columns, and it very likely survives from the era of the Jefferson Highway.

FRANKLIN COUNTY

After traveling south out of Rockwell on Pheasant Avenue for about 3 miles, turn west on 120th Street, follow it for 0.5 mile to US 65, and from there go south for about 3 miles. Now about 1 mile into Franklin County, turn west at 250th Street, which becomes Gilman Street, the main commercial street running through the small town of Sheffield (824 population in 1910; 1,172 in 2010). At the turn into Sheffield, fans of early culverts will want to notice on the near corner the large one, painted white and surviving from a much earlier day.

Until the state paved it in 1927, that mile in Franklin County just traversed from the county line to the Sheffield corner was, according to a November 8, 1927, article in the *Waterloo Evening Courier*, "the poorest stretch of primary road in Franklin County, one which was usually impassable during the wet weather of spring." However, other parts of the Jefferson Highway in and around Sheffield seem to have been very well attended to by local boosters. As detailed in the November 1917 issue of *Jefferson Highway Declaration*, Sheffield organized the responsibility for local road care into eight districts under the leadership of eight captains who filed regular inspection reports. How that system could produce good results was illustrated by road work done on the Jefferson Highway near Sheffield in August 1917. The headline from an article published in the *Sheffield Press* (quoted in the August 1917 issue of the *Jefferson Highway Declaration*) told the story succinctly: "Fifty Men Donate Road Work/Nearly 250 Loads of Gravel Was Placed on Our Roads Monday and Tuesday." This project completed the graveling of the Jefferson Highway between Sheffield and Hampton, the county seat of Franklin County.

Residents of Sheffield showed their enthusiasm for the Jefferson Highway in other ways, too. In 1917, for instance, the Fair Store on Gilman Street established and maintained a public restroom for the use of the highway's travelers. The *Declaration* pointed out in its August issue of that year the enlightened self-interest involved in such benevolence: "Catering to the wants of the public in such manner as this is a recognition of the principle that trade like kissing goes by favor." Soon the entire town caught the favoring spirit and established a very accommodating public tourist camp having a capacity for one hundred cars. According to the JHA's 1923 campground directory, the tourist camp featured a newly built (1921) "$50,000 memorial hall open to everybody, night and day, with ladies' rest room, shower baths, etc." That impressive memorial hall, located at 313 W. Gilman Street, originally also the city hall but now occupied by a private business, is still there (figure 22), and across the street are other buildings from that era. They present today a view on Gilman Street that considerably matches the one that motorists on the Jefferson Highway would have seen in the 1920s.

Stay on Gilman Street and follow it as it turns south and merges with County Road S43 (Chapin Road) at the south edge of town. In another 4 miles lies the very small town of Chapin, whose most noticeable feature is the gigantic elevators that stand beside the train tracks that front what once was the town's main commercial street (figure 23). That street now appears to be devoid of businesses, however, and in recent years at least one commercial building at the end of the street has suffered a nearly total collapse.

Chapin's commercial condition was not always so woebegone. Although its population had fallen to 87 by 2010, in 1925 the town boasted 275 residents and had many businesses, including some reflecting the town's presence on the highway, such as garages, gas stations, and even an automobile agency. As of 1928, however, Chapin was

Figure 22. The Jefferson Highway passed Memorial Hall (1921), which provided showers and restrooms for motorists camping in Sheffield. Photo by Scott Berka.

Figure 23. Gigantic grain elevators today line the railroad tracks and route of the Jefferson Highway through Chapin. Photo by Scott Berka.

no longer on the highway, after the state highway commission had finished paving the 10 miles between the Sheffield corner and Hampton on the present-day route of US 65. That new stretch of highway also was removed from Sheffield's main commercial street, but at least that town was still adjacent to and immediately accessible from the highway. Not so for Chapin, which clearly was hit hard by being completely bypassed. In response to petitioning by the town, in 1936 the highway commission did pave a short spur road that at least connected Chapin to US 65.

Continue through Chapin on County Road S43, traveling south for 5.8 miles until reaching 155th Street, which is also Hampton's Twelfth Avenue. Turn east here, go about 0.8 mile, turn south on First Street NW and follow it to the large public square at the heart of Hampton, the county seat of Franklin County. (In 1910, Hampton's population was 2,617; today, the number is 4,461.) According to the JHA's 1923 tourist camp guidebook, somewhere along this path into the town was "one of the best located tourist camps in the state, only four blocks from the main part of the city." As you proceed, note the long three-story brick building of Classical Revival styling on the east side of the street approaching the intersection with Second Avenue NW; this was once the elegant North American Hotel (later the Hotel Coonley), built in 1918, doubtless in anticipation of a substantial trade from motorists on the Jefferson Highway.

Much that is located today on the city square and on the immediately surrounding streets closely resembles what travelers on the Jefferson Highway once saw as they approached from the north. At the center of the square, buffered by a lawn on all sides, is the impressive Franklin County Courthouse (figure 24). Built in 1891, it's a massive Romanesque Revival structure made of red brick and limestone and featuring a central domed tower with a clock on each of its four faces and holding aloft the figure of Blind Justice. Four other classical figures— Commerce, Agriculture, Law, and Mercy—adorn the tower at its four corners. Facing the courthouse square on the north and west are a large number of commercial buildings also surviving from the early twentieth century. The building at the northeast corner of the public square, the Windsor Theater, merits separate mention. This two-story brick "opera house" and movie theater was built in 1912 and is now fully restored.

The Jefferson Highway continued on First Street NW to the southwest corner of the courthouse square and then turned east on Cen-

Figure 24. The Franklin County Courthouse in Hampton, the most ornate of the county courthouses on the Jefferson Highway's route in Iowa. Photo by Scott Berka.

tral Avenue E. In the block across the street from the courthouse to the south is an attractive city park, which includes a band shell. Then, after traveling one more block to the east, take note of two more eye-catching buildings remaining from the era of the old highway—on the right, the Hampton Public Library, a rectangular Neoclassical brick building completed in 1905 with funds provided by Andrew Carnegie; and on the left, Memorial Hall, a small brick, octagonal building in the Gothic Revival style. The latter was constructed in 1899 to honor the Grand Army of the Republic, and on the building's roof stands a statue of a Civil War soldier.

Leave the comely city of Hampton by continuing east on Central Avenue until reaching Fourth Street SE (also US 65), and there turn south and proceed for 19 miles to Iowa Falls. About 2.5 miles into this stretch the highway reaches a creek that is channeled today by a culvert but that once was crossed by a bridge. That bridge was the scene of a signal event in Iowa history: the state's first automobile fatality, occurring on September 29, 1905, when a motorist coming from the south at 30 miles per hour collided with the bridge. For many years (but no longer) the State Auto Insurance Association sponsored an "X Marks the Spot" billboard near this location that commemorated the event and besought motorists to "Think!"

For the remainder of the trek through Franklin County and then through Hardin and Story Counties, both sides of the road are covered by many very tall towers on which are mounted wind turbines with huge revolving blades. The wind farms along the highway in these counties attest to the fact that all three counties happen to lie in one of the sections of the state in which winds are the strongest. However, don't expect to see wind towers when proceeding past Des Moines and then through Warren, Clarke, and Decatur Counties. Wind strength, like principal topographical features and availability of road-building materials, appears to be one more respect in which the northern and southern Jefferson Highway counties in Iowa vary sharply. Over a quarter of the electricity in Iowa is generated by wind, mostly in counties in the northern and western sections of Iowa.

HARDIN COUNTY

Thirteen miles south of Hampton, US 65 reaches State Road 57 at the line separating Franklin and Hardin Counties. Since 1930, the highway has turned west here, gone a little over 3 miles before turning south, and within roughly another 2 miles entered into Iowa Falls on the northern extension of Oak Street. However, the original route of US 65 and, before it, of the Jefferson Highway continued straight ahead at this point for several miles on what is today County Road S45. Upon reaching County Road D15, the highway turned west, traveled another approximately 3 miles, and entered Iowa Falls on Rocksylvania Avenue, passing the former Illinois Central depot and train yards on the way.

The early promoters of the Jefferson Highway in Iowa boasted that their highway connected the state capital and the county seats of eight of the nine counties through which the highway ran.[1] The one exception was Hardin County, whose county seat is Eldora, a small town located in the eastern part of the county that prevailed over Iowa Falls for that honor in the nineteenth century. However, with a population of 2,797 in 1910 and 5,238 in 2010, Iowa Falls has remained the largest city in the county and therefore also one of obvious commercial importance. It is also an exceptionally attractive city, located as it is in an unusually scenic setting of canyons and rocky bluffs on the Iowa River.

The Grant Highway (later, US 20), a major early east-west route, overlapped a portion of the Jefferson Highway (US 65) through Iowa Falls, and together the highways brought large numbers of motorists into the commercial center of the city.

Residents were well prepared to welcome those motorists and their trade and to tout the natural beauties of Iowa Falls. According to the 1923 JHA tourist camp guidebook, the city's free campground had a capacity for five hundred cars and provided "electric lights, water, rest house, shade, free fuel, tables and benches." It also afforded immediate access to "fishing, boating and bathing in the summer and ice skating in the winter" and was located "in the heart of the city just across the street from garage, market, hotel, grocery, restaurant, and only four blocks from the main business district" (yet somehow, the blurb claimed, the campground also was able to remain "very secluded").

At Rocksylvania Avenue's intersection with Main Street, the highway turned south and proceeded to Washington Avenue, the city's main commercial street. Now listed in the National Register of Historic Places, the business district on Washington Avenue today preserves much of its appearance from a much earlier day and contains a good number of distinctively handsome buildings. The business on that street that was once of greatest importance to Jefferson Highway travelers—Hotel Woods—is not extant, but a café that highway travelers would have patronized—the Princess Sweet Shop, now known as the Princess Grill and Pizzeria—is still there at the same location, 607 Washington Avenue (figure 25). Established in 1915, the original Princess was destroyed by fire in 1935 and replaced in that year by a two-story building housing twenty-four booths and a twenty-five-foot soda fountain counter. The new building was a spectacular specimen of Art Deco design; among its features and appointments, as noted in its individual listing in the National Register of Historic Places, are a facade of black Carrara glass and "pitco" metal trim, a large vintage neon sign, and an interior featuring two-toned walnut booths, mirrored panels, and black Formica tabletops with white metal edges. The Princess Grill and Pizzeria retains an extraordinarily high level of integrity and should be a definite stop for all fans of the Jefferson Highway, commercial archeology, and Art Deco design.

After proceeding west for two blocks on Washington Avenue, the highway turned south at River Street, crossed the Iowa River on the River Street Bridge, and then encountered a railroad crossing so steeply

Figure 25. This Art Deco treasure, originally called the Princess Sweet Shop, is located near the earliest Jefferson Highway route through Iowa Falls. Photo by Scott Berka.

pitched that drivers going in either direction could not see automobiles approaching from the other direction. That rail crossing is still there — a rare survivor of a once commonplace kind of intersection on Iowa's early highways — but the danger is diminished in this instance by stop signs on both sides of the tracks and the slow pace of trains through the city.

Crossing the tracks and continuing south, the hard-surfaced River Street changes today at the city limits to KK Avenue, a rural gravel road that once carried the old highway for approximately 8 miles on the way to Hubbard. KK Avenue can't today be followed for that entire distance because it dead-ends after 4.5 miles upon reaching the relocated US 20 (as does a 3.5-mile stretch of KK Avenue coming from the other direction). However, a brief sojourn on KK Avenue does provide an unobstructed view in all directions of the unusually flat rural landscape characteristic of this part of Iowa. On those upper 4.5 miles can also be seen several nearly right-angled turns surviving from the original highway route.

For this route south from Iowa Falls the JHA had simply appropriated a segment of an earlier auto trail known as the Des Moines, Mason City, and Minneapolis Highway, passing over selection of another road about 1 mile to the east. The JHA stuck with its choice even after the state highway commission in 1919 incorporated that other road into the state's primary road system as Iowa Primary Road No. 1, putting it high on the list for improvements. Perplexed by the JHA's continued adherence to its original route choice, in late 1921 the secretary of the Iowa Falls Community Club wrote to the JHA to ask, "Are you going to change the marking of the Jefferson over to Primary Road No. 1 south of Iowa Falls?" In his letter, which was published in the September–October 1921 issue of the *Modern Highway*, he urged change on the ground that the Jefferson "travels over about eight miles of pretty bad road."

The route that the community club secretary advocated was adopted in 1922, a choice doubtless prompted in large part by disruption of traffic due to construction of a new River Street Bridge in the second half of that year and throughout all of 1923. Thereafter the Jefferson Highway, after coming from the north and then following Rocksylvania Avenue into Iowa Falls, turned south at Oak Street, eventually crossed the Iowa River on the Oak Street Bridge, and left the city on what is today US 65. That earlier Oak Street Bridge was replaced in 1928 by a single-arch,

Figure 26. This handsome new state-of-the-art Oak Street Bridge in Iowa Falls was completed in 2011, replacing an earlier notable single-arch bridge. Photo by Scott Berka.

open-spandrel concrete bridge having, according to the state highway commission, "the longest arch span, either concrete or steel, in the state of Iowa," which meant that travelers on the Jefferson Highway (and subsequently US 65) at Iowa Falls traveled on an exceptionally beautiful bridge across an especially beautiful spot on the Iowa River. Both the 1922 River Street Bridge and the 1928 Oak Street Bridge were subsequently listed in the National Register of Historic Places, but regrettably, the Iowa Department of Transportation concluded the latter had to be replaced, and since 2011 a new tied-arch bridge stands in its stead. Like the former arched bridge, the new one keeps the river free from cluttering support piers but, unlike the earlier bridge, does so by supporting the bridge from steel arches rising above the bridge's deck (figure 26). In addition to being handsome, the new Oak Street Bridge is also "smart" in that it incorporates an elaborate monitoring system that gives continuous readings on all aspects of bridge conditions and performance.

The final major change to the highway's route at Iowa Falls came in 1930 upon completion of paving of US 65 north of the city. No longer

Figure 27. Opening in 1930, Scenic City Kabin Kamp provided gas, food, and lodging to travelers on both US 65 and US 20 through Iowa Falls. Postcard publisher not known. Author's collection.

did the highway enter the city from the east on County Road D15 and Rocksylvania Avenue; now it connected with the northernmost extension of Oak Street and stayed with that street until exiting at the city's southern boundary. Many businesses catering to auto travelers arose along this final route of US 65, both within the city and at the highway's northern and southern approaches to Iowa Falls. (From the county line north of Iowa Falls to Washington Avenue, this route also carried US 20 until that highway was relocated south of Iowa Falls in 2004.) Although few highway-oriented businesses remain from an earlier era, one major exception is the Scenic Inn, a motel that can be found on the west side of N. Oak Street just beyond the north city limits. Continuously in business as a roadside hostelry for eighty-six years, this is another place in Iowa Falls meriting the special attention of the commercial archeologist.

Scenic Inn began in 1929 as a silver fox farm, but when the farm's owners noticed the many cars passing by on the newly paved road in 1930, they quickly opened the Scenic City Kabin Kamp, consisting of six "kabins," a café specializing in fried chicken, and a gas pump (figure 27). (Residents of Iowa Falls have long dubbed their city "Scenic City.") Soon the new roadside business had twenty-six units, and by the

1970s the count had reached thirty-two, the business's name had been changed to Scenic City Motel, but the gas station and restaurant had ceased operations. Today, the Scenic Inn has twenty-four units, two of them the original "kabins" and the remainder conventional motel units. Although the structures at this motel are now vintage items, all have been kept up immaculately, and the motel remains an exceedingly attractive family-operated business. In 2012, the owners since 1979, Terry and Deb Super, turned the motel over to their son and daughter-in-law, Nathan and Stephanie Super, to continue the family's operation of the business, thus making it likely that this will remain a Super place on the old highway for many more years.

Leave Iowa Falls by crossing the new Oak Street Bridge and continue south on US 65. To get back on the original Jefferson Highway route, after traveling 5 miles and crossing the relocated US 20, turn west on 180th Street and go 1 mile to KK Avenue, the path of the old route. Follow KK Avenue south for 4 miles to 220th Street and there proceed west for 0.5 mile to K Avenue. Continue on K Avenue (which soon becomes County Road 533) for 5 miles to Hubbard.

To track the post-1922 Jefferson Highway route from Iowa Falls to Hubbard, stay on US 65. After going south nearly 9 miles, look on the west side of the highway for a small park (located about 0.75 mile past the intersection with County Road D41 and just short of 0.5 mile of the intersection with 220th Street). The Iowa DOT map's designation of this park as "rest area—limited facilities" doesn't do proper justice to it. An inscription carved in a large rock announces that this is "Logsdon Wayside Park, est. 1934." Maintained today by the Hardin County Conservation Board, this lovely park is of that earlier era's Rustic style and comprises various stone structures, a stone shelter, picnic tables, and an unusual swing set for children. It makes a contribution to the roadside that is both unexpected and delightful.

To continue on the post-1922 Jefferson Highway route, at 220th Street go west 1.5 miles to K Avenue and follow it south for 5 miles to Hubbard. From 1927 to 1930, this was also the route of US 65, but after the latter year, the highway proceeded south of 220th Street on its present route. To see an interesting roadside remnant from the early years of the relocated US 65, travel another approximately 2 miles on US 65, to where that highway meets State 175 and turns west. After making that turn, go another 0.2 mile; on the south side of the highway is a medley of bright colors (at least during summer months) em-

Figure 28. Prairie's Edge nursery is housed in a former gas station on the Jefferson Highway route north of Hubbard. Photo by Scott Berka.

blazoning an enterprise that is identified on a faded overhead sign-board as Prairie's Edge (figure 28). This is a flower and plant business, owned and operated by proprietor Jim Blair since 1995. Facing the highway amid the flowers and other plants is a much-weathered, small cottage-style structure, which Jim says housed a gas station that operated at this location from 1946 until the late 1980s and, prior to 1946, was located at the nearby intersection. Very likely the structure dates to the early 1930s. An attached back portion of the building has already begun to cave in, however, which poses a question of how much longer this artifact of the early highway can hold on.

Continue on US 65 for 1.2 miles and then turn south on County Road S33. This was the route by which the Jefferson Highway, as well as US 65, initially proceeded into the small town of Hubbard (568 residents in 1910, but up to 845 in 2010), which lies a little over 3 miles ahead. As of 1931, however, the state highway commission had moved the route to a newly paved bypass lying just outside Hubbard's western edge. Because the residents of Hubbard had protested the impending bypass strenuously, the state highway commission gave them a consolation prize—a paved spur from the highway into the town. Soon many roadside businesses were built at the intersection of that spur and the

Figure 29. A sign recently posted on the original route of the Jefferson Highway 3 miles north of Hubbard. Photo by Scott Berka.

new stretch of highway, but none from that first generation of roadside businesses remains today.

At the turn from US 65 onto County Road S33 is a recently erected large, colorful painted sign that displays the blue and white Jefferson Highway emblem and indicates that this was the highway's original route (figure 29). The Hubbard Betterment Committee arranged to have this sign made and put up there, but it's not an indication that Hubbard is still miffed about being bypassed. Instead, the sign is another bit of evidence of a growing rediscovery of the Jefferson Highway and a newfound determination of some towns on its route to cultivate this important aspect of their local histories.

Follow S33 toward Hubbard; at 270th Street turn west, go about 0.5 mile to N. Wisconsin Avenue, turn south, and continue past the cemetery to where the street leaves town and its name changes to JJ Avenue. This path through Hubbard probably didn't last long as the official Jefferson Highway route, however, because it skirted the town's business district. The probable later route stayed on S33 until reaching Maple Street, then turned west and continued until reaching N. Wisconsin Avenue, and there turned south and proceeded toward JJ Avenue and departure from town. When taking this later route, notice the brick building inscribed "19-Garage-29" at 307 Maple Street.

Improbable though it may seem today, an article in the June 28, 1929, *Mason City Globe-Gazette* announced that Hubbard had "become a mecca for tourists and historians since the election of President [Herbert] Hoover," and the Jefferson Highway not only was the conduit for bringing them into Hubbard but was itself an important part of the Hoover story. Hoover's grandfather Eli and two uncles, Henry and Dave, owned and operated farms near Hubbard, and following the death of his parents, young Herbert lived with Uncle Dave (and Herbert's brother Tad lived with Uncle Henry). Eli was buried in the town cemetery (which was passed by the Jefferson Highway, the article noted), and his grave was "one of many points of historical interest for tourists along the Jefferson Highway." Also, a tract of land once owned by the Hoovers adjoined the highway just north of the Hubbard city limits, but the biggest part of the story was this: "The Jefferson Highway running thru Hubbard occupies land formerly owned by Henry Hoover . . . who owned the 80 acres west of the highway and platted two additions to the city." More than eighty-five years after the excitement of Iowa native son Hoover's election, however, the former president's local connections seem unlikely to grab the interest of very many of today's travelers on the Jefferson Highway and to pull them toward Hubbard.

Not so, however, for the Jefferson Highway barn, which is on a farm located a short distance beyond Hubbard and reachable by going south a very short distance on JJ Avenue past where it becomes a gravel road. Situated on the west side of the road, this barn is one of the top Jefferson Highway artifacts surviving today along the entire route from Winnipeg to New Orleans (figure 30). Painted white, the barn is a mail-order, precut wood structure (Barn Plan No. 228) manufactured by the Gordon–Van Tine Company of Davenport, Iowa, and assembled in 1917 by the farm's owner, August Saaksmeier. It has a striking gambrel roof, but its most distinctive feature is the inscription painted in black on the barn's east side facing the road: "1917 / JEFFERSON HIGHWAY / FARM." Perhaps that inscription was an indication of Farmer Saaksmeier's sense of great pride in having an international automobile highway run right past his farm. What is remarkable is that the inscription has been refreshed many times during nearly a century by subsequent

Figure 30. A gravel road carried the Jefferson Highway south from Hubbard past this barn. Inset at the top is close-up view of the inscription on the barn. Photo by Scott Berka; inset photo by Mike Kelly.

owners of the farm, even though the highway ceased to run by the farm after 1930. The barn is weathering badly, however, and needs much repair. Like the Manly Hotel, this barn is a major highway artifact to whose continued existence, upkeep, and repair fans of the old highway should immediately direct their attention.

STORY COUNTY

Resume travel south on JJ Avenue. Upon reaching 305th Street, look straight ahead to a sign indicating a "Level B" road (figure 31). Although the sign also advises motorists to "Enter at Your Own Risk," the road's condition is actually not too bad. Take this road for 1 mile to County Road D65, the end of the 4.1-mile trek from Hubbard on gravel roads. Turn west on D65, travel 0.5 mile to US 65, and turn south. About 2 miles ahead is the Story County line and, after 3 more miles, County Road E18. Turn east on E18, follow it for 0.6 mile to N. Center Street, turn south, and travel another 0.4 mile to Main Street in Zearing, a small town having 461 residents in 1910 and 554 as of 2010.

Although all of the Jefferson Highway route guides showed the highway running just west of Zearing on the route followed by US 65 today,

Figure 31. Though of diminished status today, this short road segment was once part of the Jefferson Highway. Note wind turbines in the distance. Photo by Scott Berka.

the path just taken into Zearing was, in fact, the highway's route "for a number of years," according to *Community History, Zearing, Iowa*, published locally in 1956. More likely it was actually an alternative route, bringing the road in a brief loop off and then back onto the road's main trunk, as is shown in a pre–Jefferson Highway map published in 1915 in *Huebinger's Pocket Automobile Guide for Iowa*. In any event, evidence suggesting that the highway did get into Zearing is close at hand: standing at the intersection of Center and Main Streets, note the large sign painted on the east side of the building on the southwest corner (figure 32). The bulk of the sign advertises Bailey Boys soda pop, but it also identifies the JH Cafe across the top, presenting in circles the conjoined "J" and "H" as rendered in the original Jefferson Highway insignia. This was once the site of the JH Cafe, and though the café's been long out of business, its sign continues to be maintained by the building's owner today (offering evidence, once again, that there is a growing awareness of and interest in the Jefferson Highway along the old highway's route).

Like the residents of Hubbard, folks in Zearing began agitating in the 1930s for a paved road that would connect their town to the highway's main line, but they fell far short of Hubbard's early success in that regard. Not until 1951 did the state highway commission complete a paved extension of Zearing's Main Street west to US 65. This is the main road in and out of Zearing today, but don't take it now. Instead, proceed one block north of W. Main Street to 508 W. North Street to visit the Blattel-Britton Rock & Sculpture Garden, definitely a must-see attraction while in Zearing. A wonderful concoction of plants, flowers, rocks, and fantastic metal sculptures created by two local artists, this

Figure 32. This painted sign, still maintained on the side of a long-closed business, suggests that the Jefferson Highway once came through Zearing. Photo by Scott Berka.

is another great art garden along the way, adding to the pleasures to be derived from searching out the old route of the Jefferson Highway in Iowa.

To continue traveling on the old highway route, keep going south on Central Street for 0.6 mile to 140th Street, a gravel road. Turn west, travel another 0.6 mile to US 65, and follow it south for approximately 7.5 miles. At 210th Street, stop and look at the south face of the concrete fence post standing on the southwest corner (figure 33); once again, there are the conjoined letters, "J" and "H," embossed in the concrete—one more small bit of surviving evidence that the Jefferson Highway once did run this way and that that fact mattered to people living along the highway.

Resume traveling, and within 2 more miles, arrive at Colo. Small town though it has always been (463 residents in 1910, although substantially increased to 876 in 2010), Colo once played an outsize part in the saga of the Jefferson Highway, and in recent years it has regained that large importance in the gathering movement to revive awareness and preservation of the old highway and its roadside. Colo's very location on the highway gave the town special standing: it was here that the Jefferson Highway, coming from the north, met the celebrated Lincoln

Figure 33. A concrete fence post on US 65 south of Zearing yields more evidence of the Jefferson Highway's route. Photo by Scott Berka.

Highway and then, turning west, stayed with the Lincoln for 7 miles to Nevada (and after 1921, for 7 more miles to Ames) before turning south again.

At the northwest corner of the highway intersection, one of the earliest roadside enterprises to offer one-stop service for motorists (gas, food, and lodging) on either highway had taken full form by the mid-1920s (figure 34); this complex of businesses was the creation of farmer Charlie Reed, whose farm was bounded on the east and south sides by the highways. Eventually Reed was joined by several members of the related Niland family (figure 35) in running the gas station, café, and cabin camp, each of which initially carried the prefix "L & J" (for Lincoln and Jefferson). These businesses continued in operation for many decades, until all commercial activity ended in 1995 at what had come to be known informally as Reed/Niland Corner.

Much has happened since then at Reed/Niland Corner, however, and today Niland's Café and the six-unit Colo Motel are fully restored to their appearance in the early 1950s and are both back in business. For the past five years, both businesses have been in the expert and

Figure 34. Beginning in 1923, Charlie Reed built this roadside complex at the intersection of the Lincoln and Jefferson Highways. Postcard by Hamilton Photo Co. Author's collection.

Figure 35. Charlie Reed and nephew Clare Niland. In the late 1930s Charlie managed the gas station and cabin camp, while Clare and his wife, Margaret, ran the café at Reed/Niland Corner. Photo courtesy of John Niland.

Figure 36. Proprietor and pie maker Sandii Huemann-Kelly at the pie case in Niland's Café. Her ample daily pie menu sometimes features gooseberry. Note the 1939 Cadillac coming out of the café wall. Photo by Mike Kelly.

loving hands of lessee Sandii Huemann-Kelly, whose appreciation of the Lincoln and Jefferson Highways is evident in the care she takes to operate a first-rate café and a modern motel that are still faithful to the spirit of their predecessor businesses on the two historic highways (figure 36). In the café, she notes truthfully, "we serve great food with a side of history," and the motel offers the opportunity to sleep in comfort in a vintage motel that nonetheless provides a great bed, flat-screen TV, and Wi-Fi connection, all at the bargain price of $50 a night.

Although it has not reopened, the large canopied bungalow-style gas station, built in 1926, has been fully restored for viewing by visitors, and elaborate interpretive narratives are presented both in the café and in a walking tour throughout the entire site. Stops on the latter tour include an enormous concrete Jefferson Highway sign that once was perched on the other side of the highway pointing north, the brick outline of the grease pit of Charlie Reed's original "filling station," and the cabin camp's original bathhouse, including entrances marked "Ladies" and "Men."

These welcome developments all have come to pass since 1998, when its last owner, John Niland, gave the historic property to the city of

Figure 37. Reed/Niland Corner at Colo today. Continuing in the distance is the shared route of the Jefferson and Lincoln Highways. Photo by Mike Kelly.

Colo. The city then applied for and received three "transportation enhancement" grants totaling more than $600,000 from the Iowa Department of Transportation and raised nearly $300,000 in matching money. The results of the expenditures and Colo's dedicated efforts are the revival of two valuable local businesses (figure 37), a big boost to tourist travel through Colo, and the preservation of a major historical property. Indeed, in this last regard, the Reed/Niland Corner project has a very special significance: it stands, along with the Park Inn Hotel in Mason City, as one of the two best efforts yet in Iowa—and maybe in all the other relevant states—to rescue a historic property on the Jefferson Highway from a close call with extinction. Like the Park Inn Hotel project, it offers a valuable model of what might be done elsewhere and of how to go about doing it.

Colo, the final point on this tour of the northern leg of the Jefferson Highway in Iowa, is also the starting point for the presentation of the highway's next phase in chapter 6, which resumes coverage of the Jefferson Highway route through Story County with an account of Charlie Reed's close encounter with the Iowa State Highway Commission.

6 ||| Looking for the Highway
Colo to Des Moines

The closing of Niland's Café in 1991, followed by the shut-tering of the Colo Motel in 1995, left the buildings at Reed/Niland Corner in Colo in a parlous state. For the next half decade those buildings stood unoccupied and lacked any prospects of further use, their rapid deterioration and even demolition looking increasingly probable; in-deed, John Niland pondered an offer by a Hollywood movie studio to let the buildings be destroyed in the filming of the tornado scene in the movie *Twister*. Then the unlikely happened, when, accepting John Ni-land's generous offer, the city of Colo took ownership and revived both the buildings and the businesses, making Reed/Niland Corner once again a scene of roadside commercial activity.

This was not the first time, however, that the businesses at Reed/Niland Corner had faced great peril yet managed to avert extinction. The earlier threat originated with an action—ultimately unsuccess-ful—taken by the Iowa State Highway Commission to construct a state-of-the-art interchange between the Lincoln and Jefferson High-ways at their intersection in Colo. The account of the Jefferson Highway through Story County resumes with a review of this episode, which is then followed by a look at two other major projects undertaken on the highways earlier by the highway commission several miles west of Colo. All of these projects—both the successful ones and the failed one—point to the great importance the highway commission attached to the fact that Iowa was, as its *Service Bulletin* (February 1919) put it, "where the nation's greatest east and west and north and south highways join on Iowa soil in Story County."

STORY COUNTY (CONTINUED)

That first threat to Charlie Reed's businesses began (or at least became fully apparent) in early 1934, when the Iowa State Highway Commis-sion contacted Reed to negotiate the purchase of 5.22 acres that he owned on US 30 located directly across from his businesses at Reed/

Niland Corner and that the commission alleged were needed for high-way development. At that same time and for the same reason, the commission also approached Margaret Hicks, Reed's neighbor at the northeast quadrant of the intersection, to secure the purchase of 5.88 acres that she owned lying directly across US 30 in the southeast quadrant of the intersection. When neither Reed nor Hicks would agree to sell, in April 1934 the highway commission initiated condemnation proceedings against both properties.

The highway commission had big plans for the development of the two US highways at Colo. Its first objective was to alter the route of US 65 so that, coming from the north, the highway would continue south at this intersection instead of turning west and moving coterminously with US 30 to Ames before heading south toward Des Moines. The commission also planned to construct a grade separation that would carry the new route of US 65 under US 30 at this point of their crossing. Finally, 0.25 mile south of the intersection another underpass was scheduled to be built that would take the route of US 65 under the tracks of the Chicago and North Western Railway.

An important component of these plans was the replacement of right-angle turns between US 30 and the newly extended US 65 by long, gently curving segments connecting the two highways, and for this, the highway commission claimed, the Reed and Hicks properties were needed. But why, both property owners countered, was the highway commission seeking not just the relatively small portion actually needed for building the curved segments but also the much larger triangular portion enclosed by the original highway routes and the curved segments? For both owners, this question had special salience, because in 1930 the highway commission, as it completed the paving of US 30 and US 65, had built identical curves on their properties in the northern quadrants of this intersection. On that occasion, however, the highway commission had taken no more land than the swaths—less than one hundred feet wide—needed for construction of the curved segments. Left standing in the triangular areas were, respectively, Charlie Reed's businesses at Reed/Niland Corner and Margaret Hicks's house.

Left standing, yes, but that earlier encounter with the Iowa State Highway Commission had nonetheless had real costs for both Reed and Hicks. Once that earlier road project was finished, Hicks found that she now had to cross a highway when walking the short distance from her back door to the outbuildings and fields of her farm. Reed quickly recognized that construction of the new curved segment would mean that his gas station would no longer be situated on US 65. Rather than lose that source of business or build a new gas station at a new location, he hired a firm in Boone, Iowa, to perform the laborious and expensive task of moving his station nearly 0.25 mile to the point where US 65 now met US 30. The *Nevada Evening Journal* of September 29, 1930, reported that the job had begun that very day.

These earlier experiences would probably have made both Reed and Hicks apprehensive about any further dealings with the highway commission, but the commission's new quest for much larger portions of their properties doubtless greatly magnified their concern. If the highway commission's grand project required the acquisition of so much of their land bordering US 30 to the south, they could reasonably have wondered, might the commission eventually also have designs on the equivalent portions — not pursued in 1930 — of their properties on the north side of US 30? Indeed, might the construction of those earlier curved connecting roadways have been the first phase in a grander scheme whose resumption by the highway commission was now at hand? In any case, believing the highway commission's claims against their properties to be illegal takings, both Reed and Hicks resolved to resist the commission's proceedings against them.

If Charlie Reed had had any suspicions that clearing his businesses out of Reed/Niland Corner was part of the highway commission's plan, they were confirmed early in 1935 in a conversation his lawyer, John Cross, had with C. E. Walters, an assistant attorney general representing the commission. According to Cross, as stated in a February 2, 1935, letter to Reed, Walters claimed that "what they [the highway commission] wanted to do was make a settlement with you that would involve your moving the oil station out of the intersection on the North side so that the entire intersection would be cleared out. He wants you to figure over what you think you should have in the way of damages for all of the ground inside of the curved road both North and South of the Lincoln Highway [then, US 30]. This, of course, would involve moving the oil station and tourist camp out of there and locating it somewhere else."

From Walters, Cross also learned why the highway commission assumed that Reed would quickly want to reach a reasonable settlement. First, the rerouting of US 65 would deprive Reed of customers traveling on that highway (and this, of course, would be the second time Reed had to deal with that problem). Of even greater consequence for Reed's operations, however, was a projected reconstruction of US 30 at Reed/ Niland Corner. As Cross related Walters's account, the highway commission "expected to raise the Lincoln Highway about four feet where it passes your station, the idea being apparently to go back to the high ground on the Hicks land about opposite their corn crib and carry the Lincoln Highway along on that level until it gets pretty well past the intersection so as to give more headroom for [US] 65 where it goes under [US 30]." In other words, in order to secure the needed clearance of US 65 below US 30, the highway commission contemplated such a major reconstruction and elevation of the latter highway at Reed/Niland Corner that Reed would find it impossible to carry on his businesses there.

Assuring Reed that the highway commission not only had the right to reconstruct the highway in this manner but could also secure condemnation of his property for use for this purpose, Cross suggested that Reed's objective should be to "get a decent settlement with them without having to put in too much money in court costs." He recommended that his client "get three or four pencils and start figuring, giving yourself the benefit of the doubt on various items of damage." Reed rejected that advice, however, and directed his lawyer to prepare his case for trial. In a separate suit, Hicks also prepared to meet the highway commission in Story County District Court.

There, in an outcome that must have startled even their lawyers, the plaintiffs prevailed, and they did so again when the highway commission appealed to the Iowa Supreme Court. Just as Cross had doubtless advised, however, the plaintiffs' claim that the commission was attempting to take more land than was needed for its grand project was quickly dispatched in both courts. In the district court, Judge O. J. Henderson wrote as follows: "All of the distinguished highway engineers testifying on the subject were agreed that, under the compelling necessities of modern high speed traffic, this intervening ground area should be taken over, cleared, and for all time to come controlled by the Highway Commission. . . . I am not prepared to overrule their seasoned judgment in such matter. Indeed, I am fully persuaded of the appropriateness and necessity of such taking, and of the extreme importance of the unimpeded ownership and control of both of these tracts by the Commission." Judge Henderson also rejected two procedural objections made by the plaintiffs.

But Reed and Hicks had put forward a fourth proposition, having to do with the meaning of a word found in the Code of Iowa, and this gambit took the two courts away from matters of highway engineering and into their more customary interpretive domain. The specific provision directed that, in the construction of primary roads, no ground could be "taken for the rounding of a corner where the dwelling house, lawn, or ornamental trees connected therewith are located at such corner, except by consent of the owner." Both Reed and Hicks owned houses (although neither lived in them) in the contested triangles near the corners of their properties, and both claimed that the highway commission was wrongfully pursuing "roundings" in the absence of their consent. The highway commission responded that it wasn't "rounding corners" but legally taking entire plots of land on which it would then construct curved roadways. Concluding that these truly were "roundings" as defined by the code, however, and also that the highway commission's reasoning would permit it to elude the limitation on roundings in every instance, both courts ruled for Reed and Hicks and issued the injunctions that they sought. Probably few roadside entrepreneurs have since been as fully successful as Reed in thwarting major highway projects.

In his opinion, Judge Henderson observed that "the record evidences very clearly the importance of this improvement and of the proposed relocating of No. 65. It may seem unfortunate that the Commission's plans should be balked in this manner at *the most important primary highway intersection of the entire state of Iowa* [emphasis added]. But the Highway Commission is a creature of the Legislature and under legislative control, and to the Legislature it owes implicit obedience." In its opinion on March 17, 1936, affirming the decision of the lower court, the Iowa Supreme Court agreed that "the remedy in this case, if remedy is needed, lies with the legislature and not with the court."

The highway commission never sought a change in the law, however, and simply abandoned the pursuit of its plan requiring use of the Reed and Hicks properties. The full features of that plan are not known, but two exhibits submitted by the highway commission at the original trial indicated how the thinking of the commission's engineers was tending: "Cloverleaf plan of construction at highway intersections" and "Circular plan of construction at highway intersections." The circular, or rotary, plan doesn't jibe well with the construction already done in 1930, but the cloverleaf plan not only fits perfectly with that earlier work but would account for the decision to separate the highways at different grades. It could also explain why the highway commis-

Figure 38. Charlie Reed's entire roadside operation survived the construction of this grade separation of US 30 and US 65 at Colo in 1938. Postcard by Hamilton Photo Co. Author's collection.

sion wanted that extra land inside the triangles at the corners: that was where the intricate interior roadwork could be done that would allow motorists coming from either direction on either of the highways to turn in either direction onto the other highway safely without crossing the path of oncoming traffic or even necessarily having to stop.[1] If this had been the highway commission's goal, the result would have been a great engineering feat embodying the latest in highway design and fully befitting what was, in the view of both the Story County District Court and the highway commission, "the most important primary highway intersection of the entire state of Iowa."

Although the highway commission was unable to carry out its plan in full, by 1938 it had rerouted US 65 and completed several related projects. Mere spindly arms running along the corridor of US 65 now connected that highway and US 30, not anything as grand (and space filling) as the long, sweeping curved roadways matching those on the north side of US 30 originally envisioned by the highway commission. However, a newly built underpass now carried traffic on US 65 under the nearby railroad tracks, and a new grade separation also took that highway under US 30 (figure 38). An impressive engineering achievement, the latter was also significant as one of the highway commission's earliest efforts to control traffic at the intersection of two highways by putting those highways at different grades; until then, the commission had generally used grade separations when highway and railroad tracks crossed.

These early highway features and the adjacent commercial structures at Reed/Niland Corner together make this northeast tip of Colo, Iowa, one of the top sites on the route of the Jefferson Highway, well worth a thorough inspection. When the time has come to move on, however, start west on Story County Road E41, a stretch of highway of considerable historic significance. Laid out along a section line, E41 follows the path of a road that was in place as early as 1875 and paved in 1929 at its present width of twenty-four feet. From 1926 to 1962, this road was US 30, and prior to that time, it carried both the Lincoln and the Jefferson Highways.

After proceeding for 4 very straight miles, E41 suddenly bends to the south and quickly arrives at an underpass. Go through the underpass and then immediately pull off to the left of the highway and stop on the gravel road going east that begins there. DO THIS VERY CAUTIOUSLY! The traffic moves fast here, and because the highway beyond this point abruptly turns again, this time to the west, the lines of sight are very short in both directions.

The highway's deviation from the section line previously followed is short-lived, continuing only for about a mile to the west before the highway is once again back on a path along the same section line. This deviation is of long standing, as the 1875 Andreas map of Story County reveals; any road running through these parts, both then and later, had to contend with some nasty topographical obstacles caused by the drainage system of East Indian Creek, which cuts north and south here. This site presented a problem to the Chicago and North Western Railway, too, whose route, as it proceeded west from this point, shifted from south of the wagon road to a line running north of it. Further complications came when the Chicago, Rock Island and Pacific Railroad built a north-south line through this site. In consequence, by the opening years of the twentieth century, traffic moving west on the wagon road first had to cross the North Western's busy tracks and then immediately traverse a rickety-looking viaduct that bridged both the creek and the Rock Island tracks.

Then came the era of the Lincoln and Jefferson Highways, bringing a greatly increased flow of traffic through this unusual site. However adequate the viaduct may have been for slow-moving animal-drawn vehicles, it certainly wasn't so for the ever-increasing number of automobiles now using those highways. For the same reasons, the rail crossing east of the viaduct posed increased dangers of collisions. In fact, it's impossible to look at photographs of those two early roadside features and not be terrified by what they show. The highway commission apparently felt the same way and placed the amelioration of both problems very high on its "to-do list."

The highway commission's first secured improvement was the construction of the stone-walled underpass, which was completed in 1918 and took the two highways on a much safer passage under the railroad tracks (figure 39). Until then, the highways had proceeded east from here on the gravel road shown for about 250 yards and then turned north to cross the tracks; once across, they turned east again, but the exact path they then followed north to connect with the section-line road is no longer known. To cross the tracks, motorists going in either direction first had to make a sharp left turn and then immediately climb a steep incline, conditions that made it nearly impossible to see approaching trains until their automobiles were almost on the tracks (figure 40). By eliminating this virtually blind crossing, the underpass ended a standing invitation to certain disaster.

The underpass and gravel road present a scene today virtually unchanged from that of nearly one hundred years ago. A small bit of evidence that the Lincoln Highway, prior to construction of the underpass, had indeed briefly followed the gravel road is an "L" embossed in the concrete fence post standing at the entrance to a farm just past the underpass. Until a few years ago, a painted blue, white, and black "JH" emblem was still barely visible on each wall of the underpass, but this evidence that the Jefferson Highway had also once come this way is no longer discernible.

Located immediately west of this point was the early viaduct that local road officials had built over the Rock Island tracks and East Indian Creek. In 1916 the highway commission described it as "a poorly constructed combination of wood and steel," a judgment visually confirmed in photographs made by the commission at that time (figure 41). Looking jerry-built, fragile, and unsafe, the viaduct also had a wood-planked floor that rose dangerously at a fairly steep grade from either end toward a high midpoint and then descended precipitously. Although the highway commission had targeted the viaduct for early replacement, the project was slowed first by the intervention of World War I and then

CHAPTER SIX

Figure 39. After this underpass west of Colo was built in 1918, the Lincoln and Jefferson Highways no longer followed the road shown leading off to the right or made the dangerous railroad crossing to which that road led (see figure 40). Photo by Bob Stinson.

Figure 40. Until 1918, the route of the Lincoln and Jefferson Highways made this nearly blind railroad crossing several miles west of Colo. Photo courtesy of Iowa DOT.
© Copyright Iowa Department of Transportation. All rights reserved.

Figure 41. Until 1925, this scary structure carried the Lincoln and Jefferson Highways over railroad tracks and a creek west of Colo. Photo courtesy of Iowa DOT. © Copyright Iowa Department of Transportation. All rights reserved.

by the need for the commission to secure the agreement and cooperation of the county and the Rock Island line before proceeding. Having to make do at first only with patching up the viaduct, by 1925 the commission had finally secured its replacement by a much safer reinforced concrete structure, which was then replaced in the mid-1970s.

When resuming the trek west on E41, take note of how fully the once difficult, scary, and even dangerous passage through this unusual point of confluence of creek, highway, and railroad lines has today been supplanted by a design permitting easy and safe movement without any letup in speed. Then proceed for 3 very straight miles to Nevada, the county seat. Nevada had 2,138 residents in 1910 but was up to 6,798 as of 2010.

At the eastern edge of Nevada, County Road E41 becomes Lincoln Way, and shortly beyond are several roadside remnants left from this street's earlier days as US 30 and, before that, the Lincoln and Jefferson Highways. On the south side of Lincoln Way is Starbuck's Drive-In, still in business today, but it's all that remains from the much earlier Starbuck's roadside emporium that once provided one-stop service—gas, food, tourist cabins—to motorists. A bit farther ahead, but on the north side of the street, Cook's Cabins also once offered these same roadside services. No parts of that very early business are still open today, but

Figure 42. This representation of Lincoln, but none of Jefferson, adorns the route of the Lincoln and Jefferson Highways through Nevada. Photo by Scott Berka.

the cabins remain, put to other residential use, and so does the early gas station building, now housing R&M Automotive, an automobile repair business.

Keep traveling west until reaching 1135 Lincoln Way; in the front yard is a large carving from a tree stump of Abe Lincoln wearing his stovepipe hat (figure 42). This whimsical bit of folk art is of recent vintage, but it bespeaks the significance that folks in Nevada continue to attach to the town's place on the Lincoln Highway. In every year since 1984, Nevada has also held a three-day celebration called Lincoln Highway Days, and painted on a building near the county courthouse is a large mural featuring the Lincoln Highway.

Local boosters once touted their good fortune in having a second great highway meet the Lincoln Highway in Nevada. As reported in the December 1917 issue of *Jefferson Highway Declaration*, "The Nevada Commercial Club entertained, with an oyster supper, in honor of the Jefferson Highway, Thursday, November 15. The Nevada people feel that they occupy a unique position [although it was actually one shared with Colo] in the highway development of the country by being at the crossing point of the two big highways of the country, the Jefferson and the Lincoln. This fact was emphasized in the after dinner talks and some . . . wanted to exploit it to their material advantage, and action was taken at the meeting looking to an immediate move to do so." That was then, however, and even though the routes of those two highways (and subsequently US 30 and US 65) continued to coincide in Nevada from 1915 to 1938, it is a sad fact that no murals, signs, or parades celebrate the Jefferson Highway there today.

The Jefferson Highway originally continued west on Lincoln Way past Sixth Street, Nevada's main commercial street, to what is today the westernmost entrance (now closed) to the cemetery located on the west side of Nevada. The highway turned south there on a road through the area currently occupied by the cemetery and came out at the intersection of I Avenue and W. Fourth Street. It then continued south on W. Fourth Street (Story County 620th Avenue) out of Nevada. Today, however, the cemetery road no longer goes all the way through to the city streets at the south end, and at the north end, a chain closes off the entrance from Lincoln Way onto the cemetery road.

Although this original route through the Nevada cemetery is no longer available for travel, the route that soon became the JHA's official route is. To follow it, turn south off Lincoln Way at Sixth Street and go three blocks to I Avenue. On the way, be sure to note the substantially intact early twentieth-century commercial district that occupies three blocks on Sixth Street and is listed in the National Register of Historic Places; notice, too, the Story County Courthouse (this is a replacement of the one that was here in the early twentieth century, but a handsome modern structure nonetheless); and look very closely at the former Story Hotel, now a private residential building, located on the southeast corner at Sixth Street and J Avenue (figure 43). Built in 1925 at a cost of more than $100,000 raised by subscription by local boosters, the Story Hotel met the need for high-grade accommodations for the mounting numbers of travelers on both the Lincoln and the Jefferson Highways. The Nevada Historic Preservation Commission has highlighted some of the significant features of the Story Hotel: "A combination of Mission Style and Craftsman Style, it is a well preserved example of a commercial building in a style more commonly associated with domestic buildings. The hotel had a full dining room behind the lobby. The short mansard roof is covered with metal tile. The entrance is still covered by the original metal canopy."[2]

Figure 43. The former Story Hotel was built in 1925 to accommodate increasing numbers of travelers on the Lincoln and Jefferson Highways through Nevada. Photo by Scott Berka.

Arriving at I Avenue, turn west, proceed to W. Fourth Street, and turn south to leave Nevada. Lying ahead on the original Jefferson Highway's route to Des Moines are four small towns, two in Story County—Shipley and Cambridge—and two in Polk County—Elkhart and Ankeny (although Ankeny is today no longer a small town but a sprawling large commercial, industrial, and residential satellite of Des Moines). To reach Shipley, go south almost 3 miles on W. Fourth Street, which becomes County Road S14 (also Story County 620th Avenue), and upon arriving at 260th Street, turn west and go 2.5 miles to Story County 595th Avenue. This intersection is at the southwest corner of Shipley, a town that actually appears never to have been much more than a small cluster of houses; it had ten residents in 1925 and the same "estimated number" in 2010.

Despite Shipley's very small size, however, it was for most of the twentieth century the site of a school for a large rural district. That school has long been closed, but the large, solidly built, handsome school building still stands out massively in the local landscape at the

Figure 44. From its opening year, the Jefferson Highway passed by this beautiful (but remote) former school building in Shipley. Photo by Mike Kelly.

northeast corner of the intersection of 260th Street and 595th Avenue (figure 44). A cornerstone inscription indicates that it was built in 1916 (an addition was made later), so the earliest travelers on the Jefferson Highway would also have seen this school.

Leave Shipley by going south on 595th Avenue, a gravel road (figure 45), for 4.5 miles to where pavement begins. Then continue for 2 more miles to Cambridge, a town of 696 residents in 1910 and 827 in 2010. Be sure to notice the beautiful tree-enshrouded rural Iowa scenery through which this brief last segment of the road passes on its way to Cambridge. There 595th Avenue becomes Fourth Street, and from it, go south at Water Street, the town's main commercial street. Although no trace remains of the Tomlinson Hotel that once served travelers on the Jefferson Highway, on Water Street many other early twentieth-century buildings still stand in Cambridge's small commercial district. At the south end of Cambridge, Water Street becomes Story County Road R70, which briefly jogs west before turning south and leaving the town. Within several miles, the old Jefferson Highway route will exit Story County.

Figure 45. This undulating rural gravel road, still strewn with some original concrete culverts, conveyed the Jefferson Highway south of Shipley. Photo by Scott Berka.

POLK COUNTY

From Cambridge, follow R70 (Story County 585th Avenue) south, crossing State Highway 210 after 1.5 miles and, after another mile, reaching the Polk County line. There the road's name changes to NE White Oak Drive (Polk County NE Forty-Second Street). After driving several more miles, turn east on 150th Avenue, go 0.5 mile and then turn south on NE Forty-Sixth Street. Go another 3 miles to Elkhart, where NE Forty-Sixth Street becomes N. Grant Avenue. In 1910 Elkhart was an exceedingly small town of 132 residents, but by 2010, thanks to its close proximity to Des Moines, it had more than quadrupled its size to 683. Lost in the town's transition from the early twentieth century is any obvious evidence of Elkhart's ever having been a stop on the Jefferson Highway. However, on the main commercial street Jerry's Garage does hold forth in a building that must have had a similar occupant in that earlier era.

To proceed from Elkhart to Ankeny, go south on N. Grant Avenue to 126th Avenue and turn west. (The original route would have gone as far south as NE 118th Avenue before turning west, but a golf course blocks that route today.) After traveling a little over 3 miles on 126th Avenue, turn south on NE Twenty-Second Street (which soon becomes NE Delaware Avenue) and go 3 miles to NE Eighteenth Street. Turn west there and go 1 mile to US 69 (Ankeny Blvd.). After turning south on US 69, travel 1 mile to W. First Street and follow it west for five blocks to SW Cherry Street. Turn south and go two blocks. This is the west end of the old commercial center of Ankeny on SW Third Street. Today this is a charming business district, very nicely spruced up and occupied by specialty shops. Several blocks to the east on this street a hotel once awaited travelers on the Jefferson Highway, but today neither the hotel nor its building remains.

In incorporating the Nevada-Shipley-Cambridge-Ankeny route into the Jefferson Highway, the JHA passed over an alternative route that would have taken the highway from Nevada to Ames, the next town west on the Lincoln Highway, and then have gone south to Des Moines by way of Huxley and Ankeny. The route chosen was 9 miles shorter than this alternative, but the decision turned mainly on a judgment that, of the two options, the selected route was the one in better condition. Proponents of the losing route continued to agitate for inclusion in the highway, however, which put steady pressure on the towns on the chosen route to improve it and maintain it well. Under the leadership of the Nevada Commercial Club, Nevada and Cambridge soon undertook to put down gravel on the entirety of the route in Story County, a goal achieved by the end of 1917. Merchants in Cambridge raised over $2,000 for this project, an enormous contribution from so small a town.

From the Polk County line through Ankeny, however, improvements didn't come as fast as they did north of that line. In an exchange of letters in September 1917 with JHA general manager Clarkson, a resident of Cambridge described the Polk County segment as "the rottenest stretch of road between Des Moines and Minneapolis" and charged Jefferson Highway boosters in that county with failing to keep up an agreement with Story County boosters to gravel the Polk County segment of the highway. The disgruntled letter writer added that he had recently driven on the offending highway segment "to see if it were possible to get through. We finally got through but it kept all the grown folks busy hanging onto the children to keep them from jolting out over the sides of the car." He concluded by noting that he could now understand why a traveler on the Jefferson Highway referred to in the exchange of letters had "slipped around by way of Ames when they arrived in Nevada [that is, to follow the alternative route to Des Moines]."

By the fall of 1919, however, the Jefferson Highway, including the "rottenest stretch," was now almost totally covered with gravel from Des Moines to Nevada, according to the report of Mrs. C. C. Loomis of Des Moines. Mrs. Loomis drove that entire segment on November 19, 1919, and then continued that same day from Nevada to Cedar Rapids on the Lincoln Highway. In an account published in the *Cedar Rapids Evening Gazette* on November 22, she reported finding both highways in good condition "most of the way," but there were a few "soft spots," even in portions of the roads that had already been worked on; as it happened, one place on the Jefferson Highway "proved to be the worst of the entire trip." The *Gazette* article summarized Mrs. Loomis's account: "It was about six miles south of Nevada and in what was formerly evidently a marshy stretch of ground. Ponds of water and deep mud holes bordered the roadbed and even encroached on it so that there was but a single track which was safe. But even this was impassable. Approaching the spot with caution, Mrs. Loomis saw a small car mired in the tracks with the driver unable to extricate it by its own force. Mrs. Loomis did not say what make it was, but that it was small enough to be easily pulled out with a rope fastened to another car."

Even as its small-town boosters struggled diligently to get the official route into consistently good condition for driving, others continued to advance the case for making the alternative route the official one. Although the latter's favored route was longer than the chosen one, it did have the advantage of avoiding those interminable turns in the road far out in the remote Iowa countryside. Their cause benefited greatly, too, from the fact that, because Ames was the location of Iowa State College (today, University) and also of the Iowa State Highway Commission, a good road connecting Ames to Des Moines, the state capital, had strong support from other quarters as well and had already brought substantial improvements in the road. Part of the old Des Moines, Mason City, and Minneapolis Highway, this segment was also incorporated into Iowa Primary Road No. 1 as of 1919. Add to all of the foregoing the very effective leadership on this issue by Parley Sheldon, a JHA activist and official living in Ames. A Civil War veteran, frequent mayor of Ames, and builder-owner of the Sheldon Munn Hotel there, Sheldon was also a passionate and forceful advocate of the cause of good roads. In addition to being an active member of the JHA at both the national and state levels, he was the local consul in Ames for the LHA and ultimately succeeded in his quest to have four named highways pass through Ames—the Lincoln and Jefferson Highways and the Wilson and Custer Battlefield Highways.

Sheldon's success with respect to the Jefferson Highway came in 1921, when the JHA board of directors voted to replace the original route with the alternative routing via Ames; Sheldon then made the route change official in Iowa by registering it with the Iowa State Highway Commission. Thereafter, the Jefferson Highway came west 7 miles from Nevada to Ames on the route of the Lincoln Highway and then followed the present-day route of US 69 south 8 miles to Huxley. In Huxley, the highway turned east at W. Fifth Street, south on Main Street, west on E. First Street, and south again for 11 miles on present US 69 to Ankeny, where the highway then picked up its original routing.

To resume traveling on that original route, continue south from Ankeny on SW Cherry Street for 0.3 mile to SW Ordnance Road. Turn east on this street and follow it for 0.7 mile as it angles southeast toward US 69. From this intersection with US 69, the Iowa State Capitol Building on Grand Avenue in Des Moines is 8.8 miles away, and to reach it via the route of the Jefferson Highway, first turn onto US 69 and stay with it as it soon becomes NE Fourteenth Street and, upon reaching Des Moines, changes to E. Fourteenth Street. Ankeny was once a spatially separate town (its 1910 population of 445 had soared to 45,582 by 2010), but today commercial buildings fill up the intervening space on both sides of the highway reaching from Ankeny into Des Moines. Probably none of these buildings dates from the Jefferson Highway era; in fact, most seem to be of even more recent vintage than the highway boom years of the 1950s and 1960s, although a close inspection might turn up something of interest from that earlier era. In any event, this portion of the route has none of the rural look it once had when it was part of the Jefferson Highway and is also not likely to gladden the heart of either the fan of the early roadside or the traveler searching out the old highway today.

Continue on US 69 (E. Fourteenth Street) to Washington Avenue, turn west, and continue several blocks to E. Twelfth Street. From this point, the view along the route of the old highway improves greatly. Proceed south on E. Twelfth Street through a very attractive old residential neighborhood that is also favored by a beautiful canopy of tree branches

Figure 46. The original Jefferson Highway route in Des Moines passed by the Iowa State Capitol Building. Photo by Scott Berka.

high above the street. Soon thereafter, upon reaching Grand Avenue, note the Iowa State Capitol Building straight ahead, another beautiful sight that once adorned the route of the Jefferson Highway through the central part of Des Moines (figure 46).

Des Moines was the capital of Iowa and the state's largest city (86,368 residents in 1910; 203,433 in 2010), so both the local chamber of commerce and the Greater Des Moines Committee were stunned to learn in 1913 that Des Moines would not be on the route of the Lincoln Highway. In response to this affront, the committee, according to a November 18, 1915, article in the *Des Moines Register and Leader*, "has arranged for the erection [at Ames, Nevada, and Jefferson, all on the Lincoln Highway] of signs pointing out the way to Iowa's capital. The signs also will show a map of the highways from the Lincoln road to Des Moines so there is no chance that a tourist could lose his way." Accompanying these signs would be others "advertising the hotel facilities of Des Moines and pointing out that a continuous journey connecting with the Lincoln Highway in Omaha can be procured." In other words, the intention was to lure travelers off the Lincoln Highway to Des Moines by pointing out that, after spending some time (and money, too, of course) in Des Moines, they then could resume the trip west via the Great White Way, an early named highway that was the forerunner of US 6 in western Iowa, and reunite with the Lincoln Highway in Omaha.

Once it was certain that the Jefferson Highway would come through Des Moines, the Greater Des Moines Committee's pursuit of this scheme intensified. In late November 1915 the committee's secretary announced a plan to raise $100,000 to be invested in improvements of the highway in Des Moines. As described in Greene's *Iowa Recorder* (November 24, 1915), the money would first be used to try once again to get the LHA to bring its highway through Des Moines, but if that effort failed, then the money would be spent on hard-surfacing the new highway in Des Moines, especially that portion leading north toward the connection with the Lincoln Highway at Nevada or Ames. If that large amount of money was ever achieved, certainly it didn't bring about a re-routing of the Lincoln Highway. However, hard-surfacing of the route did come very quickly thereafter. By the close of 1916, the Jefferson's route running north of Grand Avenue through the inner city to the city limits was fully paved, and so was the highway's route running from Grand Avenue via Sixth Street toward the city's southern border (figure 47). By 1920, the pavement had been extended north to Ankeny and south to the Warren County line.[3]

To follow that route south out of Des Moines, go west on Grand Avenue to E. Sixth Street and turn south. Continue 3 miles on E. Sixth Street, crossing the bridge over the Des Moines River, to Indianola Avenue, which eventually becomes Indianola Drive. Originally, the entire stretch was called Indianola Road, and motorists were instructed to follow it all the way to the city's southern edge, which today extends to the intersection of County Line Road and US 69.

This original routing of the highway to the south took motorists on Sixth Street at grade across the tracks and operations of four railroads. To remedy the congestion and ensuing traffic and safety problems, the highway later was put on a different route in Des Moines. Thereafter, upon coming into Des Moines from the north on E. Twelfth Street and turning west onto Grand Avenue, the highway continued to SW Seventh Street, headed south across the railroad district by means of the Seventh Street viaduct, and proceeded from there on Indianola Avenue, soon connecting with the highway's original path in south Des Moines (figure 48).

Figure 47. Because Des Moines was Iowa's capital and largest city, the route of the Jefferson Highway there was soon paved, as shown in this early (ca. 1920–1925) postcard view. Postcard publisher not known. Author's collection.

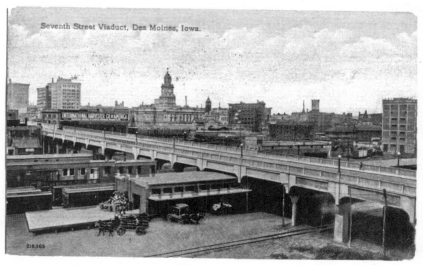

Seventh Street Viaduct, Des Moines, Iowa.

Figure 48. A revised route of the Jefferson Highway used the Seventh Street viaduct (not extant) to get over four railroad lines running through Des Moines. Postcard publisher not known. Author's collection.

This became the official route in 1920 following the completion of paving of the north end of Indianola Avenue all the way to the Seventh Street viaduct. However, well before it was paved, it appears to have been favored by some JHA officials, who already promoted it as the Jefferson Highway route in Des Moines. Indeed, as early as 1916, when certain JHA members in Des Moines wanted to erect a life-size statue of Thomas Jefferson in the city along the highway bearing his name, they proposed to place it on Indianola Road at the south end of the Seventh Street viaduct. An account of this project in the *Des Moines Register and Tribune* (copied in *Jefferson Highway Declaration* in January 1917) described this as the route of the Jefferson Highway, no doubt reflecting its actual unofficial usage for that purpose even then.

No viaduct now stands at SW Seventh Street, the last one at this location having been taken down in 1999, nor did a statue of Jefferson ever go up there or anywhere else on the highway in Des Moines. Even the JHA begged off supporting that project financially, citing more pressing highway-related commitments. According to the newspaper account, "A general subscription policy probably will be adopted. All the prominent Democrats in the city will be asked to donate and others who would like to help will not be turned down." The article then identified some of those Democrats (E. T. Meredith prominent among them, of course) behind this effort. But perhaps here was exposed a fatal flaw in their quest for money on behalf of commissioning and erecting the statue: going beyond linking the proposed statue to the highway, its promoters sought also to use the statue as a commemoration of the founder of the Democratic Party. They were heedless, apparently, of what impact this might have on fund-raising prospects in a state that was then very solidly Republican.

To depart from Des Moines, proceed from the intersection of US 69 and County Line Road on US 69 for 1 mile to where US 69 and US 65 merge and then continue south on those highways toward Indianola. The pursuit of the old route of the Jefferson Highway has now moved out of Polk County into Warren County and also begins a trek through a completely different landscape, as recounted in the next chapter.

7 ||| Looking for the Highway
Des Moines to the Missouri Border

Early promoters of the Jefferson Highway sometimes put a happy spin on their accounts of the highway's passage through southern Iowa by shifting the focus away from the highway's many sharp turns, steep climbs, and precipitous descents to the natural beauty of the highway's setting—the "Adirondacks of Iowa," according to a puff piece appearing in the November 1922 issue of the *Modern Highway*. Speaking in Osceola, Iowa, on September 12, 1929, Hugh Shepard, former JHA president, indicated how the Jefferson Highway's early advocates actually viewed the region, as reported the next day in the *Mason City Globe-Gazette*. The occasion was a celebration of the completion of paving of the highway from Des Moines to Lamoni—a joyful all-day event that included a caravan of nearly one hundred automobiles moving between those two cities, a ribbon-cutting ceremony held just north of Indianola, and many speeches along the way made by local magnificoes and JHA leaders. In his speech, Shepard presented a brief account of the good roads movement in Iowa and then confessed that, in the JHA's earliest days, "we referred to southern Iowa as the 'darkest Africa' of the Jefferson Highway."

Shepard was not the only northern Iowan to find motoring in southern Iowa to be a distinctive experience. Franklin Jaqua, editor of the *Humboldt [Iowa] Republican*, recounted in the September 5, 1924, issue of his paper a trip he had just made on the Jefferson Highway from Iowa Falls to Kansas City. Of the portion of the trip from Des Moines to the Missouri border, Jaqua wrote the following: "It was in southern Iowa that we began noticing the little differences in the ways of the people and their mode of life. Most noticeable was the method of road building. There was no gravel south of Des Moines, and as one neared the Missouri state line the grading and dragging became poorer and poorer. The lay of the land also changed materially. Hills were more frequent and their surfaces had been cut down less. At one moment you were at the peak of a hill and at the next were struggling through a valley. There was more timber, fewer clean pastures, and corn became poorer and poorer."

As Jaqua's last sentence recognized, the respective landscapes along the highway north and south of Des Moines differed in economic as well as topographical features. The northern region's unending open fields, planted with corn and other bountiful crops and occupying some of the most productive agricultural land in the world, quickly yielded south of Des Moines to a variegated economic landscape of thick stands of trees, hillside pastures, coal mines, and less productive cropland laid out in smaller fields. The three southern Jefferson Highway counties— Warren, Clarke, and Decatur—are part of the Southern Pasture region of Iowa, one of five agricultural regions of Iowa identified by historian Lowell Soike, while Polk County and the other counties to the north through which the Jefferson Highway proceeded are situated in the North Central Grain region. A long-standing consequence of their different economic circumstances has been a lower per capita income for people in the two southernmost counties, Clarke and Decatur, than for the Jefferson Highway counties north of them.[1]

As he went south past Des Moines, Jaqua also concluded that "even the citizens seemed to change character," becoming more "suspicious" of strangers. Whether or not that was so, a region so different economically and topographically from its counterpart counties north of Des Moines was likely also to have some distinctive cultural features. The Works Progress Administration's *Guide to the Hawkeye State* found one—raccoon hunting, "a favorite sport in this region of heavy growth virgin timber"[2]—and devoted half a page to laying out the main features of this arcane pastime. Fox hunting also had a following in southern Iowa, and one rallying place for that activity's devotees, called the Log Cabin, was located on the Jefferson Highway halfway between Indianola and Osceola. Were jackrabbits also a favored target of hunters in southern Iowa? In any event, a resident of Leon found a novel way to dispatch one of the long-eared critters in an unusual human-rabbit encounter on the Jefferson Highway, as recounted in the *Leon Reporter* (and copied in the *Hamburg [Iowa] Reporter* on December 5, 1929): "Edward P. Griffith, of southeast of Leon, while driving on the paving north of Leon, Sunday evening, ran down a big jack rabbit, which tried to outrun his Chevrolet car, and when the car finally struck Mr. Jack Rabbit, it was all over. Edward was exhibiting the rabbit in Leon Monday, which was one of the largest ever seen in this vicinity."

For Shepard, however, the "darkest Africa" characterization was confined to the many early impediments to easy motoring on the Jefferson Highway in southern Iowa and the slow pace at which they were surmounted. But surmounted they were at last; passing bond issues for the finance of road improvements and working closely and systematically with the state highway commission throughout the 1920s, the three southern counties actually beat the northern counties by a whole year in completing the paving of their portion of the highway. In recognition of that achievement, Shepard, according to the newspaper account, referred to an assurance made by locals in 1916 at the outset of the campaign to build the Jefferson Highway that southern Iowa had "caught the spirit." "I'm pleased today to find," he concluded, "that you good people have delivered on your pledge to build good roads."[3] More than eighty-five years later, it's still possible to obtain from traveling the route of the Jefferson Highway from Des Moines to the Missouri border a good sense of the magnitude both of the problem those early road makers faced and of their achievement in transforming an uncertain path into a modern highway.

WARREN COUNTY

Today, most of the 10-mile drive from the Warren County line to Indianola can be done with great ease at 65 miles per hour on the divided lanes of the two conjoined highways US 65 and US 69. Four miles into that drive, however, be sure to slow down enough to get a good look at the Hastie gas station situated on the west side of the road (figure 49). Built at this location in 1933 by Indianola resident Ross Hastie, this small brick building housed a Standard Oil gas station of the "domestic" type; outside were a grease pit and two gas pumps (those there now are replacements). After closing in 1943, the station stood unoccupied and neglected for many decades until the Warren County Historic Preservation Commission took custody of it and made the restoration of this important remnant from an earlier era on the roadside a long-term project.

Easy as it is to drive this gently graded and smooth-surfaced stretch of road today, in the Jefferson Highway's earliest days the going was much tougher. One of those early drivers lamented the steep hills (then) between Des Moines and Indianola and the challenge of getting "through, over, and across the bluffs of Middle River," a substantial

Figure 49. The Hastie Station, closed since 1943, is located 4 miles south of Des Moines on US 65/US 69. Photo by Scott Berka.

natural feature located about 5 miles south of Des Moines. "Unless very careful when you are boasting about good Iowa roads," he concluded ruefully in a June 3, 1921, article published in the *Alden [Iowa] Times*, "somebody is likely to take the joy out of life with a mention of [the roads of] Warren and Lucas counties."

One can today see along the east side of US 65/US 69 (about a mile past the Hastie Station) some of the challenge identified by that early motorist: the road bringing the highway to Summerset, the first town on the Jefferson Highway south of Des Moines, departed from the highway's main line, the Indianola Road, by turning east into what is today a low area occupied by Banner Lakes and Summerset State Park but formerly the Banner Coal Mines. Then, after continuing south and crossing the Middle River, the road proceeded toward the small town. Once the highway had gone through Summerset, it turned to the west and was soon back on the mainline route to Indianola.

Summerset today appears to be little more than a collection of houses mostly arrayed for a mile or so along Summerset Road, the main access road from US 65/US 69, but even in 1910, it was a very small town of

Figure 50. The Jefferson Highway (*at left*) originally crossed railroad tracks (*at right*, now a bike path) here at the north edge of Summerset. Photo by Scott Berka.

only one hundred residents. In view, too, of the extra effort and mileage needed to navigate into and out of Summerset, it was inevitable that complaints about including the town on the Jefferson Highway would arise. A letter to the editor of the *Indianola Herald* (reprinted in *Jefferson Highway Declaration*, December 1917), for instance, argued that the extra mile added to the trip between Des Moines and Indianola was costly to motorists and that newly available federal funds to Warren County should be used to build a new bridge and road bypassing Summerset. As of 1923, that new bridge and bypass had been accomplished.

Although the original routing to and through Summerset can't be followed fully today, a portion of it can. To do so, leave US 65/US 69 by turning east at Summerset Road; after 0.6 mile, turn north onto 138th Avenue and follow it to its dead end. This gravel road parallels the bed of former Rock Island railroad tracks, now a bike trail, and ends at a driveway running up to the east side of a house (figure 50). Beyond lies the chasm of the Middle River, which was once crossed by a bridge that brought the Jefferson Highway from the north to the point of access to 138th Avenue via what is now that driveway. To trace the original highway route south from this point, return on 138th Avenue to Summerset Road, turn west, and turn south at 133rd Avenue. Upon reaching Fulton Street, take a brief jog west to US 65/US 69, and there proceed south. Indianola lies 4 miles ahead.

The county seat, Indianola had 3,283 residents in 1910 and 14,782 in 2010, the large increase no doubt attributable to its close proximity to Des Moines. The outskirts of Indianola today are filled for a distance of a mile or so with the usual contemporary commercial clutter and are a far cry from the hollyhock-strewn roadside that some Indianolans sought in 1930. J. N. "Ding" Darling, the celebrated political cartoonist with the *Des Moines Register*, who was also an ardent naturalist and chair of the Men's Garden Club of Des Moines, had also thrown his heft behind that proposal for roadside beautification in Indianola, as recorded in the August 15, 1930, edition of the *Rock Valley [Iowa] Bee*. Whether or not the project was ever implemented, today no hollyhocks grace US 65/US 69 at Indianola, nor are there any other roadside features in this approach to the city surviving from an earlier era. However, look on the west side of the road for a recently built roadside attraction: the National Balloon Museum and Ballooning Hall of Fame, which, coupled with an annual national ballooning event, has brought an unusual kind of renown to Indianola in recent years.

The street bringing the Jefferson Highway route into Indianola was originally known as Second Street, but later the name was changed to Jefferson Street and, more recently, to Jefferson Way. Was this final name inspired by the designation Lincoln Way found in many cities and towns (five in Iowa) through which the Lincoln Highway ran? And if so, might this be evidence of a new stirring of awareness of the historic importance of Iowa's first north-south highway? Perhaps, but if the highway was ever in the past called Jefferson Way or even Jefferson Street through any city or town in Iowa, today that is so only in Indianola. That city therefore remains the exception proving the rule: in Iowa, the Jefferson Highway seems never to have taken the same hold on minds that the Lincoln Highway had, which helps account for why it remains a mostly forgotten road today.

At Euclid Avenue, turn west and go two blocks to Howard Street. As of 1918, the highway turned south here, but today Howard Street is a one-way street going north, so proceed another block to Buxton Street, which edges Buxton Park, the site of Indianola's former public tourist camp. The campus of Simpson College is close by, and originally the Jefferson Highway (and before it, the Interstate Trail) actually followed a route running by Buxton Park and then around the college campus, adding unnecessary mileage to the highway. Indianola's decision in 1917 to shorten the route through the city drew the praise of the JHA, which commended the decision "to the thoughtful consideration of several other towns on the Highway similarly situated" (*Jefferson Highway Declaration*, December 1917). Shortening the route through towns and cities was a constant major preoccupation of the JHA, but one not always shared by local commercial interests.

Turn south on Buxton Street and continue five blocks to Salem Avenue; then go east one block to Howard Street to the southeast corner of Indianola's public square, site of Warren County's courthouse, which faces Salem Avenue. Although not the courthouse building that was here during Jefferson Highway days, the present building is a handsome one well worth a close look. Built in 1938–1939, it presents both Art Deco and Moderne design features and is one of ten county courthouses in Iowa whose construction during the New Deal era was funded by the Public Works Administration (PWA).

Before Howard Street was made into a one-way street going north, motorists seeking to follow the old Jefferson Highway route could proceed south from Euclid Avenue for five blocks through Indianola's commercial center to this point. To continue following the highway's route south, proceed east from this point for two blocks to Jefferson Way and then turn south on US 65/US 69. After several blocks, note on the east side of the highway the old Woods Motel, a remnant from an earlier era that is still in business as the Woods Motel & RV Parking.

Immediately after reaching the southern edge of Indianola, US 65/ US 69 makes a steep descent of 0.7 mile, crosses South River, and then ascends for 1.8 miles. Here is the first instance of a physical feature to be encountered many more times on the route of the Jefferson Highway between Indianola and the Missouri border. Well aware of the burdens that driving in hilly terrain imposed on drivers, the JHA tried to make light of them, as in the following note published in the *Jefferson Highway Declaration* in December 1917: "People have gone to great expense in city amusement parks to erect a system of chute the chutes. No such expense is necessary on the Jefferson Highway between Kansas City and Des Moines. Nature has already made them." Continuing, the short pronouncement maintained that "it is mighty exhilarating 'Shooting the Chutes' of the Jefferson Highway. The fun of the thing soon gets in

Figure 51. Nature is steadily reclaiming this abandoned section of the Jefferson Highway route south of Indianola. Photo by Scott Berka.

one's blood and we predict the attraction of the sport will draw hundreds of people, living in flat countries, to tour over the Berkshire Hills of the Jefferson Highway." Facetious though the statement was, it implicitly recognized that motorists were likely to find much of the going challenging on the Jefferson Highway in southern Iowa.

Just after completing its ascent, the highway reaches McGregor Street. Turn east, go 0.1 mile, and arrive at a segment of the original late 1920s paved highway (eighteen feet wide, curbs still intact) that is today identified as 130th Avenue. Go south here for 0.2 mile to a gate blocking further access. Beyond this gate is about one more mile of the original paved road, unused after its abandonment circa 1946 and fully encroached on by the growth of trees and other vegetation over the subsequent years (figure 51). Today this is private property, however, so any exploration would need the consent of the owner.

Return via McGregor Street to US 65/US 69 and proceed south 1 mile; then turn east on Nevada Avenue and go 0.1 mile to 130th Avenue, which is a continuation of the old highway from the south end of the blocked-off portion. This is another very short early highway segment, which can be followed from this point for 0.2 mile north or 0.3 mile south, in either case ending at a barricade. Return to US 65/US 69 via Nevada Avenue and resume traveling south on a road featuring numerous curves, steep hills, and equally steep descents. Stay on US 69 when very shortly it parts ways with US 65.

At this point of divergence, US 69 moves diagonally in a southwest direction for 24 miles to Osceola on a route that for most of the way approximates the original one but no longer has the original's many right-angle turns and steepest grades. This route was made part of the Jefferson Highway in 1915 by virtue of the fact that it had been incorporated into the Interstate Trail in 1911. In choosing that route, the Interstate Trail Association had passed over two alternative routes, as described in a May 25, 1911, article in the *Chariton [Iowa] Herald Patriot*. One of those routes left Des Moines by way of Norwalk and Martensdale and continued south over the route traced today by County Road R45 to Osceola. The other followed today's US 65 south through Lucas County and into Wayne County past Humeston to County Road J20 and, turning west there, arrived at today's US 69 about 6 miles north of Leon. The first alternative, however, traversed the west side of Warren County, thereby missing Indianola, the county seat; and the second option not only failed to reach the county seat of either Lucas or Wayne County but also left Osceola, county seat of Clarke County, off the route.

The route selected ensured that, of the two counties covered by the route (Warren and Clarke), the county seats of both would be served by the highway, and this very likely was the reason for its selection. Otherwise, it's difficult to see any other solid reasons for including this route in an interstate highway. Only three other towns—Cool, Medora, and Liberty—were on the route between Indianola and Osceola, all very small then and no more than clusters of houses today. True, the route chosen (and followed by US 69 today) suggests a hypotenuse and probably was shorter than the alternative routes by a few miles. However, that consideration fails to take into account that this road had to work its way through some of the most challenging terrain in Iowa, sometimes following ridges but sometimes holding to paths laid out by section lines or used as wagon roads in the nineteenth century. The latter features ensured that the highway would often proceed in halting fashion, making many angled turns and incorporating many dizzying roller-coaster loops that were not fully eliminated until this part of the highway was fully paved in 1929. No doubt the two options not chosen would also have presented problems for road building and driving—this was southern Iowa, after all—but it's hard to believe that either could have been any more challenging than the route chosen.

From the point at which US 65 and US 69 separate, follow the latter for about 3 miles to 120th Avenue (a gravel road), turn south, and proceed 2 miles to Cool—or at least what used to be Cool, a town always so small that it often was omitted from early maps and that today consists of three houses. Continue on 120th Avenue, which at this point becomes a wider gravel road. Then, after another 1.2 miles, the road makes a sudden precipitous descent, which is followed by a long, very steep climb to the road's previous altitude (figure 52). This is the most pronounced undulation remaining in the original Jefferson Highway route in Iowa and conveys a good sense of the rigors that once confronted early motorists on that highway (in the earlier era it was a dirt road, too, not even having the advantage of its present gravel surface). By relocating the highway, the state highway commission avoided the massive job of having to cut the grade and fill the hollow here, but its engineers still had to contend with plenty of hills and dales elsewhere on the route of US 69.

Stay on 120th Avenue and, within another mile, turn west on County Road G76, a paved road. Follow it for a mile to the intersection with US 69. Note the remains of the Medora store, no longer in business. Medora lies straight ahead on G76 past the intersection, but not much is left of the town today other than a church and some houses.

Once, however, Medora was a community full of pep, proud of its place on the Jefferson Highway, and eager to upgrade its portion of the highway. In early 1917, at a meeting held in the Medora schoolhouse, seventy local and nearby residents agreed on needed improvements in the highway and raised over $250 to get started on them. According to a later newspaper report, by the end of 1917 a fund of several thousand dollars had been raised and spent on the road improvements. The December 1917 issue of *Jefferson Highway Declaration* carried high praise from JHA headquarters for Medora's efforts and results: "For years Warren County in the vicinity of Medora has been afflicted with a nightmare known as the Cow Path, which was supposed to answer the purpose of a road. One day the Jefferson Highway came that way and the exhaust from many mufflers woke Medora. As soon as Medora followed the biblical injunction, to have faith, a mighty work was per-

Figure 52. This short stretch of the original Jefferson Highway route northeast of Medora illustrates the challenge that once faced road building in southern Iowa. Photo by Mike Kelly.

formed there and now people are no longer referring to the Medora Cow Path but are talking about the Medora miracle. People are going for miles to see this piece of wonderful new road."

Whatever those improvements were, however, they were only a start, leaving a lot more work still to be done; indeed, the 3 miles between Medora and the road's entry into Clarke County continued to be regarded as the most challenging and dangerous section of the entire Jefferson Highway in Iowa. The problem was that the JHA was attempting to make use of a stretch of road whose path through a very difficult terrain had been laid out in pre-automobile days. The specific nineteenth-century route from which JHA hoped to wrest an automobile highway is disclosed in a 1902 map of the Medora area (figure 53); note the numerous turns needed in order to advance even several miles. An early motorist described this portion of the highway well: "The road angles and turns in every direction, as many as twenty turns being noted within a distance of three miles, while some of the approaches are dangerous because of the narrow highway and the many narrow bridges and numerous hills" (*Chariton [Iowa] Herald-Patriot*, July 20, 1916).

In May 1924, the Warren County Board of Supervisors decided to spend the county's share of the state primary road fund on construction of a new road from Medora to the Clarke County line, and the project was put on the state highway commission's docket for the next year. In a January 14, 1925, letter to Hugh Shepard, Fred White, the highway commission's chief engineer, discussed, among other items, "the famous [he meant infamous, of course] Medora link at the south edge of Warren County" and the need to do something about it. "This short stretch of road," White wrote, "about three miles in length, has for years been the terror of motorists on the Jefferson Highway. Immediately to the southwest of the little town of Medora this road climbed a very steep hill. On the side of this hill there was a right angle turn. Many wrecks occurred at this point due to the inability of drivers to make the turn, and many deaths resulted." But the highway commission had just let contracts, White noted, to relocate that road, eliminating the old road's dangerous turns and steep grades. "In a year from now," he predicted, "the traveler of the Jefferson Highway will find a fine broad highway with easy grades and long, sweeping curves substituted for the old crooked road with steep grades."

In fact, the road was done even sooner, as proclaimed in a headline

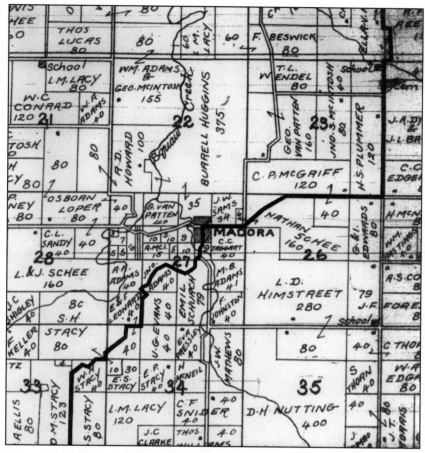

Figure 53. Map depicting the tortuous original route (*dark line*) of the Jefferson Highway through Medora. Each large numbered square represents 1 square mile. From *An Atlas of Warren County, 1902* (Knoxville, IA: Hovey & Frame, 1902).

in the August 20, 1925, *Osceola Sentinel*: "New Medora Road Open. Hills and Sharp Turns Eliminated in Fine New Highway." The new stretch of highway became part of US 69 in 1926 and was paved as of 1929. To follow it today, simply turn south from County Road G76 onto US 69 and go 3 scenic and easily traversed miles to the Clarke County border. And don't bother to look for the old "Cow Path" road; the street that once carried it south out of Medora dead-ends today at a creek after several hundred feet, a continuation of the road very far beyond that point is not evident, and much of the land the old road would next have run through has been reconfigured today as Hickory Hill Park, which is maintained by the Warren County Conservation Commission.

CLARKE COUNTY

From the county border, travel 1 more mile to Liberty, another town no longer indicated on maps and no more than a cluster of houses today. Until several decades ago, however, Liberty did have a general store, a small, low wood-frame structure located on US 69 at the intersection with County Road R59, the road moving south from Liberty. Today only traces of the foundation of the store remain. However, when it was in business, the store bore a hand-painted sign so unique and charming that it would be wrong to let it slip into the past undocumented and forgotten (figure 54).

From the Liberty corner, go 10 miles on US 69 to Osceola, noting the many posted 35- to 40-mile-per-hour curves encountered on the way. The curves make the going slow here, but not nearly as slow as when many of those curves were angled turns. The state highway commission worked steadily in the early 1920s to eliminate sharp turns along the entire route of the highway through southern Iowa. The success of that effort and its welcome payoff in easier driving were testified to by a motorist, Chicago banker F. C. Upton, in the January 13, 1927, issue of the *Humboldt Independent*. There Upton happily reported finding that "there is not a square corner on the Jefferson Highway between Des Moines and Leon, Decatur County. Every square turn has been eliminated." Upton was further gratified to discover that this specific portion of the highway "between Indianola and Osceola, for a long stretch follows a ridge and a magnificent view is afforded on either side. Tracts of timber along the way add variety and beauty." Iowa newspapers from that era contain other testimonials by motorists to the great natural scenery found along the Jefferson Highway here and elsewhere in southern Iowa. Of course, motorists' enjoyment of the section's beauty was bought at the price of having to proceed more slowly and cautiously here, even after completion of the highway commission's improvements, than was required of motoring on the highway in northern Iowa.

In 1910, Osceola, the county seat, had a population of 2,416, but by 2010 that number had grown markedly to 4,929. Upon entering the city, look on the west side of the highway for a large model of the Statue

Figure 54. In Liberty, this choice bit of folk signage at the Liberty Store (not extant) once graced the Jefferson Highway route. Photo by Bob Stinson, 2000.

of Liberty. This hard-to-miss icon stands in the spacious yard of a very early motel originally known as the Klemme Motel but today called the Homestyle Inn. A little farther ahead on the east side of the highway are the remains of another very early roadside hostelry, the Elms Plaza Motel. Although called a motel, this place was actually a tourist court consisting of a grouping of multi-unit small houses. The Elms Plaza is no longer in business, but its vintage roadside structures are still there, now converted to other residential uses.

In the first half of the 1920s, before motels and tourist courts had made their appearance, Osceola, like many other towns and cities on the Jefferson Highway in Iowa, maintained a free public tourist camp for the overnight accommodation of motorists. Unlike most municipal tourist camps, however, the one in Osceola was set up within a block of the city square rather than at a city park or other city-owned open land located away from the heart of the city. Taking note of this unusual fact, in the November 1922 issue of the *Modern Highway* the JHA general secretary described Osceola's as an "artificial" construction, "conceived by the good ladies of the different clubs" and having, in addition to its central location, other "conveniences that have been added [to] make up for the natural advantages of other camps." Among those conveniences were electric lights, showers, a screened dining room, a kitchen equipped with coin-operated gas stoves, a yard coated with gravel (to hold back the mud), a car wash, and sheds for cars.

Having a capacity for forty cars, the tourist camp appears to have been well used. Registration data published in the *Osceola Sentinel* of October 5, 1922, indicated, as the *Modern Highway* later reported, that "more than 1,000 people were registered [at the camp] between August 9 and September 18" in 1922 and that they came from "practically every state in the union" and from Canada. To see where the tourist camp was located, continue south on US 69 toward the city square and go one block west to the easily spotted city water tower; the camp occupied an open area in front of the tower where the US Post Office now stands.

By the time the Jefferson Highway came through Osceola, the city had a well-developed business district built up around a central square where the county courthouse stood. Lining that square today are many handsome commercial buildings remaining from that earlier era, such as the recently restored old Masonic lodge building on the east side of the square and the Lyric Theatre and the former Hotel Garner on the square's west side (figure 55). Sad to say, however, the old courthouse— an imposing brick beauty with a high clock tower—that had stood at the center of the square since 1892 was taken down in the early 1950s because some of the bricks were deteriorating but also, according to the county's website, because the county had "outgrown" the old building. Regrettably, its 1956 replacement—a two-story, L-shaped building— falls short of the scale, distinction, and charm of its predecessor.

From the city square, continue south on US 69, noting on the east side of the highway near the junction with US 34 the Blue Haven Motel, a vintage motel still in business. From the intersection, begin a 9-mile trek to the Decatur County line and the turnoff to Weldon. Coming up soon after departure is a very steep descent in the highway, and shortly into that descent, at the south edge of Osceola and on the west side of the highway, is the Clarke County Historical Society's headquarters and museum. Among the museum's many treasures is an original porcelain and steel Jefferson Highway sign bedecked with "Pine to Palm" inscription and imagery.

Several miles south of Osceola, the highway ascends again. A well-known postcard photo taken in the 1930s from the ascent's high point and looking back toward that city shows the long sweep of the highway

Figure 55. The route of US 69 (the Jefferson Highway) along the east side of the city square in Osceola, shown in the 1930s. Today, the buildings are little changed. It is still the route of US 69, but the street bricks are covered and cars no longer park in the middle of the street. Postcard by L. L. Cook Co. Author's collection.

through rolling hills and pastures (figure 56). A shot taken today from nearly that same point shows a similar scene (figure 57), differing from the earlier photo mainly in revealing a greater presence of trees along the highway and the absence of a low fence and several billboards that once adorned the highway. From this point to the Decatur County line, the highway remains fairly straight in alignment, but many thrilling up-and-down undulations occur on the way.

Near the Decatur County line, notice the Mormon Pioneer Trail sign, one of several posted along US 69 at places in this area where the highway intersects or runs close to the main nineteenth-century Mormon trail to the west (figure 58). Also, at the intersection with Clarke-Decatur Road (County Road J12), look for Wade's Café, which has offered food and gasoline at this location since the 1940s and is a rare survivor from a time when many such businesses flourished along US 69. Then go east for 2 miles on Clarke-Decatur Road (County Road J12) to the small town of Weldon, which straddles the line separating Clarke and Decatur Counties but falls within the exclusive jurisdiction of the latter county.

Figure 56. On a postcard from the 1930s, a beautiful view, looking north, of the Jefferson Highway (US 69) south of Osceola. Postcard by L. L. Cook Co. Author's collection.

Figure 57. A view of the Jefferson Highway (US 69) today, taken from a location close to that used in figure 56. Photo by Scott Berka.

Figure 58. For about 10 miles south of Osceola, the Jefferson Highway (US 69) route is straight and in places flat. Here, near the Decatur County line, the highway briefly coincides with the trail the Mormons followed west in the mid-nineteenth century. Photo by Scott Berka.

DECATUR COUNTY

Although Weldon was 2 miles off the route of the Jefferson Highway, it was listed in the JHA route guides from the start, probably because there were no towns on the highway available to provide services to motorists on the 20-mile stretch between Osceola and Leon. Once a bustling town, Weldon has undergone much change since the era of the Jefferson Highway. In 1910, the town's population was 308, but as of 2010, that number had fallen by more than half to 125 residents. Further evidence of Weldon's decline is the apparent absence of any viable business there today. Among its vestiges of former economic activity are a small gas station today housing the town's public library; an old brick building once serving as the local post office but now vacant; and a collapsing former service station at the entrance to town. But several charming features of the town do remain, including a wooden sign on which WELCOME TO / WELDON / ALWAYS HOME fills in the

Figure 59. Standing at the head of the county road leading to Van Wert, this structure may once have provided gas and other services to Jefferson Highway motorists. Photo by Scott Berka.

space of an outline of the state of Iowa, and a nicely planted and lighted boulevard defined by parallel gravel-surfaced streets running through the town from north to south.

Return by way of the Clarke-Decatur Road to US 69 and follow it south 2 miles to County Road J14. At that intersection note the abandoned wood structure, probably once an early service garage, bearing a US 69 sign (figure 59). Follow County Road J14 west about 1 mile to Van Wert, which, like its nearby sister city of Weldon, was always listed as a Jefferson Highway town, even though it wasn't directly on the highway's route.

Van Wert has a nicely kept up and sizable residential area, but it's another Decatur County town that has lost population over the years; whereas in 1910, 461 people lived there, by 2010 that number had fallen to 230. Its commercial center has completely dried up, leaving behind a row of five crumbling contiguous brick commercial buildings (at least one is now used for affordable residential units) along the west side of a very wide Main Street, the east side of which no longer has any build-

Figure 60. A remnant of palmier days in Van Wert. Photo by Scott Berka.

ings. However, an indication that this was once a livelier commercial center is a remarkable "ghost" sign for a local realtor that fills the north end of the northernmost building and still stands out vividly in red letters against a fading white background (figure 60). Today, Van Wert happens to be located at Exit 22 of Interstate 35, the latest version of a highway linking St. Paul and Kansas City. However, if the town once was an oasis of goods and services that could draw travelers 1 mile off the Jefferson Highway, it plays no similar role for travelers on I-35. A motorist pulling off the latter highway at Van Wert today in search of fuel or a restroom would doubtless succumb to panic upon finding that not even a gas station or convenience store is there today.

Return to US 69 and proceed 9 miles to Leon, encountering many more hills and curves on the way. Also, 6 miles into that stretch (that is, 3 miles north of Leon), look for the octagon barn on a farm located on the east side of the highway at 180th Street (figure 61). Sitting atop the eight sections that make up its roof is a cupola that also has an eight-sectioned roof. Built in 1905, this unusual barn has been a noteworthy sight on the Jefferson Highway from the start.

At Leon, US 69 today runs south through the city on Church Street

Figure 61. An octagon barn, built in 1905 and located 3 miles north of Leon on US 69. Photo by Scott Berka.

to First Street and then west for about 1.5 miles before turning south again and departing the city. This was not the route of the Jefferson Highway, however, that—doubtless at the insistence of local merchants—at NW Tenth Street took a one-block jog to the east in order to move the traveler south on Main Street, thereby bringing visitors into Leon's business center.

When the route through the city was being paved in 1928, some local boosters came up with a scheme to ensure that motorists would know that Leon was on the Jefferson Highway. An article in the *Adams County Union-Republican* published on October 31, 1928, gave the details: "When the last of the concrete was being poured, just at the city limits, some of the residents of the town brought enormous wooden letters two inches thick and three feet long and persuaded the contractor to insert them in the roadway. Later these letters were removed and the places were filled with colored cement and the result will be a sign designating the town which will remain there as long as the pavement lasts." This project indicates how highly communities once valued their connection to the Jefferson Highway. If those letters are still there, however, they're now buried under another layer of concrete and no longer visible.

Having experienced some small growth in population in the twentieth century, Leon, like some other small municipalities in Decatur County, has nonetheless in recent decades begun to lose population. Whereas the city had 1,991 residents in 1910, after passage of one hundred years the count had dipped slightly to 1,977. Helping to sustain Leon, however, is its status as county seat. Look on the east side of Main Street, just past the intersection with Third Street, for the county courthouse. Listed on the National Register of Historic Places, it is described in its documentation there as "a variation on a Renaissance Revival" structure, "designed in a simplified Beaux-Arts style." Particularly striking is the building's tower, which consists of a lower open portion holding aloft four clocks facing, respectively, in the four main directions, topped off by a dome.

On the streets surrounding the courthouse are commercial buildings, some of which retain their appearance from an earlier era. In the block directly across the street from the courthouse is the South Central Iowa Theatre, known locally as SCIT and still open and showing movies on weekend nights. Also of interest is the structure located at the southwest corner of the intersection of Main and First Streets. Today known as the Mallott Apartments, in the era of the Jefferson Highway this building was the Hotel Leon, and evidence of that fact can still be found in "HOTEL LEON" painted in large letters on the back of the building by the apartment house parking lot (figure 62). When Hotel Leon was built in 1925 (replacing another one of the same name at this site destroyed by fire in 1923), the *Osceola Sentinel* proclaimed it (May 28, 1925) to be "the only modern fireproof hotel between Des Moines and St. Joseph" and well positioned to accommodate motorists arriving from what was then a full day's drive from either Mason City or Kansas City.

The original Jefferson Highway route through Leon continued south on Main Street past Hotel Leon until reaching SW Twelfth Street. Turning west there, the highway followed a curving gravel-surfaced path until reaching the road now designated as US 69. For a variant, easier-to-drive route out of Leon (and a much more plausible one for a highway carrying heavy traffic), stay on Main Street heading south until reaching Pleasanton Road, turn west to 220th Street, and then follow the latter until reaching and turning south on US 69. After traveling several miles on US 69, look on the east side of the highway for a road

Figure 62. In Leon, Jefferson Highway motorists would have seen this sign painted on the south side of the former Hotel Leon. Photo by Bob Stinson.

identified as Old US 69 and follow it to Davis City about 4 miles ahead (figure 63).

Old US 69 was a stretch of the original Jefferson Highway that was incorporated into US 69 in 1926, paved in 1929, but then relegated to the status of a county road when the present alignment cutting 1 mile from US 69 was completed in 1953. Its curbs have been removed, and it now has an asphalt surface that has sustained much cracking and erosion, but Old US 69 is still at its original narrow width of eighteen feet and, best of all, passes through a terrain of exceptional bucolic charm. Soon after making the turn, notice the great view to the west, and the beautiful rolling meadowlands and the many thick stands of trees throughout. About 1 mile into the trek at Little River is a pony truss bridge, built in 1943 and one of only two vintage bridges left on the original route of the highway in Iowa (figure 64).[4] Although it probably has been spared from replacement so far by virtue of its no longer getting much heavy use, it nonetheless is in very poor condition, and assurance of its repair and continued existence would doubtless be assisted by recognition of its historic value. The bridge and the rest of Old US 69 clearly constitute major highlights of the route of the Jefferson Highway today.

Figure 63. Old US 69 (previously the Jefferson Highway) is a charming but deteriorating 4-mile stretch of road south of Leon. Photo by Scott Berka.

Figure 64. Built in 1943 and located on Old US 69 south of Leon, this is the only remaining vintage truss bridge on the entire route of the Jefferson Highway in Iowa. Photo by Mike Kelly.

Upon reaching and rejoining US 69 at the northern edge of Davis City, note the public park off to the right across the highway. This was once the site of a heavily wooded public tourist camp, of which the town's residents and local JHA members were justifiably proud. The description of the park in the 1923 JHA tourist camp guidebook waxed both lyrical and rueful, pointing out first that the park was part of what had been, until fairly recent times, a great primeval forest. "Here the red man had his home and was shaded and sheltered by the forest growth. . . . Here the red squirrel and the honey bee had their winter home. . . . Here the Pottawatomie Indians made camp and held their pow wows." However, "such scenes are now gone forever. Where there was once beauty and the silent glade there is now the smell of gasoline and the chug-chug of the motor car. The woodman's ax and the ruthless hand of ignorance have laid waste the most beautiful forest land on the American continent." But what, if anything, could be done about the depredation? Certainly no effort to repair the damage or resist the further advance of highways and automobile usage was proposed; instead, some local citizens "set about to save the remnant of forest land adjoining Davis City. The result of their foresight saved . . . thirteen acres of primeval forest land." The town's residents and Jefferson Highway boosters now hoped many others from far parts would come and enjoy their forest preserve. In their eagerness to bring in tourist dollars, however, they apparently overlooked the likelihood that the visitors' campsites and fume-spewing, noisy automobiles would further threaten their bit of sylvan paradise.

Davis City was once an economically viable town and full of feisty promoters of the Jefferson Highway, but, like Weldon and Van Wert, it has undergone a substantial loss in population and diminution of economic well-being since those early years. Having 489 residents in 1910, one hundred years later Davis City was down to a population of only 204. Although a handful of brick commercial buildings dating from the early twentieth century still are there on both sides of US 69, few businesses, other than a tavern, remain in those buildings. In a separate wood structure located on the west side of the highway the Davis City Café is still open, but its large sign jutting out over the sidewalk is weathering badly (figure 65).

Continue on US 69, which veers off in a southwesterly direction, soon moves straight west toward Lamoni, and after about 5 miles crosses Interstate 35. From this point, Lamoni lies only 2 more miles down the

Figure 65. The Jefferson Highway, like US 69 today, went through Davis City on that city's very wide main business street (here shown looking south). Photo by Scott Berka.

road. At the intersection with I-35 is the Chief Lamoni Motel, an older independent motel whose name and colorful sign bearing an Indian motif are perplexing, inasmuch as Lamoni was a king figuring in the *Book of Mormon*, not an Indian chief. That the city has a Mormon name is not perplexing, however. In the 1870s, the city of Lamoni grew out of a settlement affiliated with the Reorganized Church of Jesus Christ of Latter-day Saints, now known as the Community of Christ. This was the branch of Mormonism that rejected polygamy and was eventually led by Joseph Smith III, son of Joseph Smith Jr., the founder of the original Church of Jesus Christ of Latter-day Saints. At first living near church headquarters in Plano, Missouri, in 1881 Smith III moved to Lamoni; his house, Liberty Hall, located at 1138 W. Main Street, is now a local museum whose holdings include a great panoramic photograph of the entourage in an early JHA sociability run. To visit Liberty Hall, stay on Main Street for several blocks past the point at which US 69 turns south on State Street.

Lamoni differs from the other municipalities on the Jefferson Highway route in Decatur County in having a seemingly more robust economy and a present-day population (2,324 in 2010) larger than its 1910 population (1,541). Doubtless one factor contributing to those differences is the presence in Lamoni of Graceland University, an institution founded by the Reorganized Church but today nondenominational, even though it's still owned by the Community of Christ.

US 69, still tracking the old route of the Jefferson Highway, comes into Lamoni on E. Main Street and soon crosses Linden Street, on which many of the downtown businesses are located. Notice that on both sides of the highway Linden Street is still paved with bricks—and until about a decade or so ago, so was this portion of the highway—but today those bricks are covered with asphalt. Follow US 69 for another four blocks, turn south on S. State Street, and, after going another 5 miles, haul up at the Iowa-Missouri border. The tour of the Jefferson Highway through Iowa is now at its end.

On the same September 12, 1929, on which he gave his speech of celebration in Osceola, Hugh Shepard stood at this point and, according to the next day's edition of the *Mason City Globe-Gazette*, "looked over into a veritable sea of mud across the state line" and saw there "a reminder of what the stretch through Warren, Clarke, and Decatur counties had been prior to the completion of the paving."[5] No longer, however, did motorists need to approach a trip through the steep hills, deep valleys, and mud of southern Iowa in a state of trepidation, as if on an expedition into threatening territory. Ever since, and as the tour just completed reveals, the trip could be done with an ease that completely subverted the notion of southern Iowa as "darkest Africa." Thanks to the leadership and perseverance of Shepard and others in the JHA, it was now even possible to enjoy fully the alleged Berkshire Hills or Adirondacks of Iowa when driving the route of the Jefferson Highway from Des Moines to the Missouri border.

Epilogue
Thinking about the Highway

Is the Jefferson Highway in Iowa still there today? And would I be able to find enough material to document the saga of the old highway? Those two questions gnawed at me as I contemplated writing this book. Now that the book nears an end, however, the pertinent questions are, what did I find, and of what consequence was the highway? I offer here a few conclusions and some final thoughts about the Jefferson Highway over its lifetime of one hundred years.[1]

The answer to each of my original two questions turned out to be yes, of course, but that answer came more quickly to the first question than to the second. One trip over the route of the Jefferson Highway in Iowa was all I needed to establish that virtually the entire original route is still there, accessible, and little changed for many decades. Many subsequent trips yielded the detailed information about the highway today presented in the three preceding chapters. From those chapters, the following few paragraphs distill the main features of the Jefferson Highway's continuing presence in Iowa.

South of Des Moines most of the old highway was simply incorporated into present-day US 65 and US 69 without much alteration of route (the exceptions are the early routings into Summerset and Leon; the short abandoned segments located south of Indianola and Leon, respectively; and the brief stretch linking Cool, Medora, and Liberty). Today, the highway is wider, it no longer has those early notorious curbs, and its many early sharp-angled turns were long ago replaced by curves, yet what remains is essentially the original highway. That highway is still laid out in two lanes, it's still posted at a speed limit of 55 miles per hour (except where curves reduce speed even further to a mere 35 or 40 miles per hour), and it still moves through residential and business streets of nearly all of the towns and cities on the route.

North of Colo, US 65 subsumes much of the old Jefferson route but does bypass several small towns that once were on the earlier route and makes several other small departures from that route. However, like its named predecessor, today's numbered highway still winds its way through Iowa Falls and three county seats—Northwood, Mason City, and Hampton—and it remains a modest two-lane road with a speed limit of 55 miles per hour all the way to the Minnesota border.

Only in the narrow section from Colo through Des Moines does the present routing of US 65 depart greatly from the route of the Jefferson Highway. Near or in Des Moines, the old route has at places been altered beyond recognition or possibility of travel. Elsewhere in that midsection of the old highway, however, are located some of the highway's most interesting unaltered miles—those that coincided with the route of the Lincoln Highway, and subsequently US 30, from Colo to Nevada (and after 1921, on to Ames). That route was spared any alteration when the highway commission in 1962 chose instead to relocate US 30 a mile to the south of the old road.

If the Jefferson's route remains surprisingly intact, that's far less so for features of the early roadside that sprang up alongside the old highway. After the passage of a century, most traces of the Jefferson Highway name or logo have disappeared, and most instances of early highway commercial activity stimulated by location on the old highway—gas stations, highway eateries, tourist courts—have also come and gone. Yet, as the preceding tour of the route in Iowa revealed, there are some exceptions, including such spectacular ones as the Park Inn Hotel, the Scenic Inn, the Jefferson Highway Farm, and Reed/Niland Corner. Although most of the small towns and cities on the route (those in Decatur County and a few in northern Iowa excepted) have grown modestly over a century, they remain small in population and retain much of their appearance from earlier days, especially those having vintage town squares. Indeed, enough of the past remains to whet the interest of any "aboveground archeologist" and to add to the sense that the old highway is still there and awaits exploration.

On my many trips taken along the highway while gathering information for this book, I always marveled at how little altered from a much earlier day are the location of the route, the characteristics of the highway, and even the charming look of the small-town settings and bucolic scenes through which the highway passes. In contrast, some other major highways in Iowa, such as US 20 and US 30, are, in piecemeal fashion, being transformed into 65-mile-per-hour, four-lane divided roads that bypass most of the towns and cities on their routes. Probably such large-scale remodeling would be harder to accomplish on a highway that courses through the challenging landscape of southern

Iowa. However, a likelier reason that little tinkering has been done on any portion of the route of the Jefferson Highway through Iowa is that Interstate Highway 35 is always nearby; following US 69 very closely most of the way through southern Iowa, I-35 is also rarely ever farther away than 10 or 15 miles from US 65 in northern Iowa. Anyone wanting to move fast to reach a town or city on the old Jefferson Highway route or to go beyond Iowa to Minnesota or Missouri can do so much more expeditiously on I-35. There has been no need, then, to make any "improvements" in the older highways running on a nearby similar route.

This, of course, means that those older highways that took over the Jefferson Highway route through Iowa have a somewhat diminished standing today, not reduced to the status of "blue highways" but still likelier to be used for local and regional travel than to serve long-distance motoring. On the other hand, the close alignment of I-35 with the Jefferson Highway route in Iowa does point to the soundness of route decisions made by the promoters of the early highway (and of the even earlier Interstate Trail); indeed, I-35 approximates the routing of the Jefferson Highway all the way from St. Paul to Kansas City. As the successor to the Jefferson Highway, I-35 also indicates that the Iowa State Highway Commission got it right when it very early identified the Jefferson Highway as the route to be promoted (as Iowa Primary Road No. 1) for conducting motorists north and south through Iowa. In sum, then, the long stretch of I-35 between St. Paul and Kansas City implicitly testifies to the historical importance of the Jefferson Highway and might even be considered the present-day embodiment of the earlier highway between those two end points.

Although interstate highways approximate large portions of the Jefferson's route in other states (sometimes very closely, as in Missouri and northwest Louisiana), over some stretches of the old highway in northern Minnesota, Kansas, Oklahoma, Texas, and Arkansas, no corresponding interstate highways are within range at all. In contrast, the Lincoln Highway is today subsumed in its entirety by one interstate highway, I-80, which follows the original route fairly closely all the way from New York City to San Francisco. This contrast hints at a basic fact of one hundred years ago: the Jefferson Highway may have been (at least initially) the main road connecting Winnipeg and New Orleans, but its routing was not always optimal. As noted in chapter 1, routing choices were sometimes made opportunistically and in response to grassroots pressure, but sometimes, too, JHA had to forgo directness of route in order to find suitable preexisting roads to incorporate into the highway.

In the JHA's campaign for the highway, however, the claim that the Jefferson Highway was the north-south counterpart of the Lincoln Highway or that it provided an improved road all the way to Winnipeg or New Orleans may not have been the most fetching claim. For people living along the highway, likely a bigger concern would have been the highway's prospects for serving more salient local or regional interests. Certainly along a 2,300-mile highway those interests were varied and numerous. Because it made possible the promotion of vacation tourism in north-central Minnesota, for instance, the blazing of the Jefferson Highway was warmly welcomed there and was followed by the creation in 1918 of the Ten Thousand Lakes of Minnesota Association (and the next year, of the Jefferson Highway Transportation Company, a regional bus company that continues today as the Jefferson Bus Lines). Lying behind all of the route controversy in Arkansas was a similar quest to have a highway that would support the big effort made there in the 1920s to advance Ozarks tourism. And for a final example, the Jefferson Highway was hailed in Iowa for such modest reasons as that it provided a link to the Lincoln Highway, facilitated tourists' access to summer vacations at Clear Lake, and made trips to the state capital much easier.

As all fans of America's early automobile highways know, however, the impact and significance of those highways reached well beyond their opening of new routes for faster-moving automobile travel. The widespread use of privately owned automobiles on greatly improved highways profoundly affected many aspects of the lives of Americans, including where they lived and worked and how they spent their time. More than simply improved corridors for motoring, early highways soon changed the "look" of America and were also, in effect, a new kind of national stage, one bringing to the boards new kinds of scenes and performances. Certainly the Jefferson Highway in Iowa provided illustrations of these new features of American life.

Not all of those new features were desirable, of course—for instance, highway accidents, of which the Jefferson Highway had its ample share. The pages of the early issues of the Iowa State Highway Commission *Service Bulletin* revealed that agency's great alarm over the mounting numbers of accidents, all of which were also documented in sometimes gruesome detail in newspapers. Contributing to the problem, in addition to often primitive roads that had not been designed for automobile usage and also intersected too many railroad tracks, were attempts by some motorists to set speed records or to engage other drivers in races. Such car races were an especially bad idea on the zigzags, steep climbs and descents, and unfinished surfaces of the Jefferson Highway in southern Iowa. An article published in the June 25, 1925, *Chariton [Iowa] Herald-Patriot* recounted the sad story of one impromptu car race on that highway north of Davis City that resulted in a crash of one of the cars and three deaths. According to a survivor traveling in the car that finally left the road and crashed, the driver perceived a challenge from a Ford roadster and announced that "he had never let a Ford pass him and didn't propose to" then.

Two already well-established American practices—bootlegging and robberies of banks and gas stations—were also given a further big boost by the early highways. The Lincoln Highway was especially accommodating of the delivery of illicit booze from distilleries in western Iowa to Chicago, Omaha, and points beyond. But the Jefferson Highway also facilitated both of the above fields of outlaw endeavor and extended them out into the Iowa countryside; for example, and as noted in chapter 5, the highway provided the Dillinger gang with fast and easy movement to and from a Mason City bank. An article published in the *Rolfe [Iowa] Arrow* on July 14, 1927, provided an amusing account of the activities and capture of a small-time bootlegger who operated along the Jefferson Highway in southern Iowa and stashed his booze in the ditch along the highway south of Indianola.

The Jefferson Highway, it appears, even accommodated the spread of the Ku Klux Klan in Iowa in the 1920s. An account published in the *Adams County [Iowa] Free Press* on September 15, 1923, described a Klan initiation ceremony, adorned by a fiery cross and presided over by frightening hooded figures, that took place along the highway north of Osceola. Automobiles brought the initiates to the remote site of the proceedings, while on one of the high hills through which the highway weaved its way the Klan found a perfect setting for projecting its frightening cross of fire far out into the countryside.

The opening of the auto trails in the early twentieth century also fueled a wanderlust that brought many people onto the highways for long-distance automobile trips having little or no conventional utilitarian purpose. Not merely vacationers, these motorists were motivated by a sense of adventure, a yen to explore, or the challenge of completing a difficult journey and being among the first to do so. Although many early motorists traveling from the east to the west coast (and sometimes in the reverse direction) published accounts of their trips, I have so far found only a few brief accounts in newspapers of trips on portions of the Jefferson Highway and no account of an automobile trip over its entire route. But perhaps not many motorists (other than the highway's early promoters on their sociability runs) ever made that complete trip. As E. T. Meredith noted in 1916, "The trend of travel since Columbus" had been from east to west, and the challenge of motoring from coast to coast—for instance, on the Lincoln Highway—neatly fit that long-established pattern. In addition, of course, the Lincoln's 3,300 miles by themselves offered a more inviting challenge than the Jefferson's 2,300 miles.

Also on the highways in those early years, usually moving on foot but sometimes by unusual motorized or animal-drawn vehicles, were many colorful characters who were there for various reasons, such as to set a record, promote a cause, restore personal health, win a cash prize, settle an election bet, solicit money donations, or simply avoid having to settle down and stay put in one place. Their zany purposes often freed their wanderings from the grip of the usual east-west pattern of such long-distance travel. For instance, when Plennie Wingo of Abilene, Texas, decided he would walk around the world, he set off on April 15, 1931, in an easterly direction. However, upon reaching Dallas, he turned north and followed the Jefferson Highway route all the way to Joplin, Missouri, before resuming there his eastward course to New York City and the start of an ocean voyage to Europe. After being harassed in Bulgaria and arrested and jailed in Turkey, however, Wingo decided to cut short the rest of his trip, and eighteen months and 8,000 miles later, he was home again. Many people had made similar treks on foot to distant parts of the globe, of course, but Wingo had a unique claim for his jaunt: he had done the entire trip walking backward, and that included all of his shipboard walking while on the ocean portions of his journey (figure 66).[2]

Poking around in early newspapers, I uncovered accounts of four more walking expeditions (all moving forward) that used the route of the Interstate Trail or the Jefferson Highway.[3] One account described the effort of three young Canadian men to win a $1,500 prize by walking from Winnipeg to New Orleans by a date certain; another article re-

Figure 66. Assisted by special glasses in his backward walk around the world, Plennie Wingo here approaches McAlester, Oklahoma, on the Jefferson Highway in 1931. Photo by Acme Photo. Author's collection.

counted the attempt of a man (whom the reporter said "appears to have a sort of fad for walking") to make that same trip in 1924, but walking in the other direction; and two newspaper stories gave accounts of trips over portions of the route between St. Paul and Kansas City that were parts of longer treks culminating on the west coast. One of those walkers was a World War I veteran, who had been "gassed over in France" and took up walking to restore his health; in 1922 he had traveled on the Jefferson Highway from St. Paul to Colo, Iowa, where he then headed west on the Lincoln Highway. Making the other trip were two teenaged boys who in 1914 set out to walk along the Jefferson's predecessor, the Interstate Trail, from Des Moines to Kansas City and then on to San Francisco. They planned to haul a homemade wagon placarded with "good roads" information and signs and also to give talks along the way on the need for improved roads, but I found no later reports indicating how far they actually got.

As roads improved and automobiles became more reliable, so-called traveling men—traveling salesmen and company representatives—began a long-term shift away from reliance on trains to use of automobiles for making their rounds. Strange to say, among the earliest to take to the highways in pursuit of a livelihood were people with disabilities who moved by means of specially adapted motorized or animal-drawn vehicles and financed their trips by selling along the way notions or postcards documenting their efforts. I uncovered a remarkable instance of a disabled motorist traveling the Jefferson Highway in the August 16, 1921, *Humeston [Iowa] New Era* (as copied from the *Osceola Sentinel*). Under the headline "Armless Genius at Osceola," the article described the travels of Fred Erickson, a Kansas City man then aged sixty, who had lost both arms in an industrial accident at the age of twenty-three but in recent years had taken to the road selling shoe laces and pencils over a territory spanning Kansas, Nebraska, South Dakota, and Iowa. When interviewed in Osceola, he had been on the road for nearly three months and had covered approximately 4,500 miles. Much of his route in Iowa was the Jefferson Highway, which was also the road he intended to follow for his trip home to Kansas City. Unfortunately, the article failed to give a good description of how this admirable man, lacking arms, was able to operate an automobile.

The most vivid of the highways' early effects was a transformation of America's roadsides by new types of businesses catering to the servicing of automobiles and their passengers. An early step in this dra-

Figure 67. The Tourist Park on the Jefferson Highway in Hampton in the late 1920s could accommodate one hundred cars and their occupants. Postcard by L. L. Cook Co. Author's collection.

matic change came during the first half of the 1920s, when a vogue for "autocamping" brought many motorists onto the nation's highways in pursuit of vacation camping trips. In response, local chambers of commerce and municipal governments everywhere eagerly created free public tourist camps, hoping thereby to entice the fast-growing numbers of autocampers to pitch their tents for the night and spend money locally.

By 1923, I discovered, seventeen towns or cities on the Jefferson Highway in Iowa—for instance, Hampton (figure 67)—had established free public tourist camps for the accommodation of the many motorists then on the road. Most of the camps along the route were very well accoutered, too, typically offering such amenities as free showers, cooking gas, and firewood. Because both the autocamps and their nomadic users were exotic new components of town life, local newspapers often took note of them, publishing summary information on the numbers, home states, and destinations of the registrants checking in at their respective tourist camps.

Ten years later, however, the craze for autocamping had long since ended, virtually all free public tourist camps were gone, and now mushrooming on roadsides everywhere were private hostelries that charged a fee but provided a room with a bed for the night. So sudden and vibrant was this development that *Fortune* magazine took account of it in a long article, "The Great American Roadside," published in its September 1934 issue. The main reason for the magazine's interest was obvious: in those dark days of economic depression, the roadside was one of the few places in which the American economy was booming. Thousands of people fortunate enough to own property adjacent to major highways had decided to try their hands at catering to the traveling public's need for gas, food, and lodging. As the *Fortune* article recounted, a gaudy new drama was unfolding on roadsides generally, and I found evidence of that along the Jefferson Highway in Iowa.

Consulting early tourist accommodation guidebooks, I determined that, by the mid-1930s, those earlier seventeen public tourist camps had been supplanted by at least thirty-three private operations in fifteen towns and cities on the original route of the Jefferson Highway in Iowa. The names of these places often were quaint, and nearly all still included the word "camp," usually prefixed by "tourist," "cabin," or "cottage"; some examples were Russell's Evergreen Cottages in Northwood, the Scenic City Kabin Kamp in Iowa Falls, the L & J Cabin Camp in Colo, the Cabinola Cabin Camp and Sells Orchard Tourist Camp, both in Indianola, and the W. C. Bagg Camp, Cross Roads Cabin Camp, Happy Hollow Cabin Camp, and Pine Crest Cottage Camp, all in Osceola. The Sylvan Motel on US 65 in Des Moines stands out as the only one of the thirty-three to use in its name the term that would eventually come to denominate all lodging facilities on America's highways. Indeed, the Sylvan very likely was the earliest and, for a long time, the only place in Iowa called a motel, a word imported from California that doesn't show up much in listings of highway facilities in Iowa until after World War II.

Many—perhaps even most—of these new places were family-run "one-stop" operations offering gas and food as well as lodging and often had much "homemade" flavor and sometimes idiosyncratic decorative touches, such as units made to look like log cabins. Yet among these early roadside businesses were three—Green Gable Cottages in Mason City, Green Gable Camp in Hampton, and Green Gable Cottage Camp in Hubbard (figure 68)—that offered the first hints of an eventual greater standardization of roadside services. In spite of the slight variations in their names, these three were parts of the earliest attempt in the United States to create a nationwide franchise chain of

Figure 68. This roadside business (not extant) on the US 65 bypass at Hubbard began as one of many franchised Green Gable cabin camps in the early 1930s. Postcard publisher not known. Author's collection.

hostelries along the principal highways of the United States. Headquartered in Onawa, Iowa, the Green Gable chain foundered in 1934 in the depth of the Great Depression, however, leaving behind and on their own more than seventy cottage camps scattered across Iowa and several other midwestern states. Not until after World War II did national motel chains finally take hold along America's highways.

The many new businesses sprouting along the nation's highways greatly facilitated long-distance automobile travel for most travelers but, regrettably, not for all. Although automobile ownership was rising fast among African Americans eager to escape the indignities they often experienced in travel by train, only rarely would they have found welcome in the new roadside hostelries. From the mid-1930s through the mid-1960s, intrepid black motorists usually found it advisable to carry with them on their trips the latest annual issue of *The Negro Motorist Green Book* or any of several other similar guides listing places where they might be served a meal or secure a room for the night. Away from large cities, however, the listed lodging options were few. As late as 1961, for instance, *The Bronze American National Travel Guide* identified a mere twenty-five tourist courts and motels available for patronage by persons of color on the entire 3,300-mile route of the Lincoln

Highway, and only three of those were in Iowa, in spite of that state having a strongly worded public accommodations law adopted in 1883. But the many guide books reveal an even bleaker reality for lodging accommodations for black travelers on the Jefferson Highway across Iowa; listings included several hotels in a black neighborhood in Des Moines and four tourist homes in Osceola, but no motels or tourist courts at any point on the highway route across the state. Certainly, too, no change in this pattern of very limited offerings was likely to occur as the highway descended into states south of Iowa, in some of which segregation was buttressed by law. Only following passage and enforcement of the federal Civil Rights Act of 1964 would persons of color begin to get the same service long enjoyed by white travelers along America's highways, including those in Iowa.

Although the early private tourist camps on the Jefferson Highway in Iowa closed long ago, latter-day versions of three are still in business. Two of those very early camps were identified and discussed in earlier chapters—the Scenic City Kabin Kamp of Iowa Falls, which continues today as the Scenic Inn; and the L & J Cabin Camp in Colo, which morphed in 1946 into the Colo Motel, closed in 1995, but reopened under that later name in 2006 as part of the restoration and reopening at Reed/Niland Corner. The third early business to still have a presence today is the Ames Tourist Court (figure 69), which was built in 1926 on the Lincoln Highway and the 1921 Jefferson Highway route through Ames, Iowa, and has been in continuous operation ever since. Still providing thirty units arranged in the original court configuration, it is known today as the Ames Motor Lodge.

The end of World War II brought the construction of some new motels along the route of the Jefferson Highway, but only a few of those remain today, such as the Royal Motel in Northwood; the Crossroads Motel at US 65 bypass at Manly; and a small handful, identified in chapter 7, in Indianola, Osceola, and Lamoni. Why are there so few motels, especially late-model ones, today along the old route? Most long-distance travel in this corridor now takes place on I-35, so that's where the newer motels are—nearly all outposts of national motel chains, not independent ventures arising from the grass roots. In sum, the curtain has closed almost completely on the roadside scene—indeed, on the very *kind* of roadside scene—once found along the Jefferson Highway in Iowa.

Figure 69. Built in 1926 on the Lincoln and Jefferson Highways in Ames, the Ames Tourist Court was likely the first in Iowa to be designated a tourist court and to replace cabins with a row structure. It is still there as the Ames Motor Lodge. Postcard by Albertype Co. Author's collection.

The highway remains, however, still testifying to the undertaking begun a century ago by many citizens widely scattered in towns and some major cities in the midsection of the United States. Their achievement was notable, but what finally can be said about the Jefferson Highway activists themselves? Some, such as E. T. Meredith, W. A. Hopkins, and Hugh Shepard, clearly had outstanding leadership ability, but otherwise the highway's partisans don't seem to have had any unique or special attributes; they appear simply to have been representative members of a prosperous but provincial business and professional class located throughout the American hinterland. Perhaps their most striking quality was a heightened sense of self-efficacy. Manifesting the "go-get-'em" spirit characteristic of that era, they were also fortified in their conviction that Americans could achieve great things by the completion of the Panama Canal in 1914.

That optimism and self-confidence found expression in "The Jefferson Highway Man," a poem written by George G. Stockard of Mountainburg, Arkansas, and published in the May 1916 issue of *Jefferson Highway Declaration*. Its first and third stanzas convey the gist of the poem:

I'm proud of the Jefferson Highway man
Who dreamed the dream and made the plan;
But here's to the boy along the route,
Who carries the dreamer's vision out.
And whether he gives his brawn and vim
Or gives his cash—here's health to him.

While other folks complain and whine.
Because there's too much rain or shine,
He gathers grapes they might have got,
Because he's Johnny on the spot.
Here's to the hustling son-of-a-gun
And here's to his family, every one.

A dreamer of lofty dreams who was also able to carry out those dreams by spotting opportunities and jumping on them, a take-charge guy but also a dutiful foot soldier, a faithful worker who was always a booster and never a knocker or a whiner—presumably these characteristics touted in the poem matched well the self-concept held by the men actually recruited to the association (there were women members, but mostly they were there as wives and adjuncts). Satirists could have found much choice material to work on in this exalted depiction.

As it happened, during those same years all Americans of the type and class of the Jefferson Highway promoters actually were subjected to much derisive commentary for their alleged backslapping conformity and narrow political, social, and cultural views. Satirized most notably by Sinclair Lewis in his 1922 novel *Babbitt*, they were also labeled and skewered in H. L. Mencken's many writings as the "booboisie." If the lampooning was sometimes heavy-handed and unfair to its targets, much was right on the mark. Moreover, in some of the words and activities of the Jefferson Highway's advocates it's easy to spot evidence of the mentality that those literary heavy hitters mocked.

Evidence is there, for instance, in the highway promoters' fondness for certain buzz words and clichés (such as "live-wire," "hustle," "boost, don't knock") favored in business circles at that time and in their zest for joining the many fraternal lodges then found in small-town America (for instance, Hugh Shepard, though entitled to wear a Phi Beta Kappa key, was also a Mason, a Knight Templar, a Knight of Pythias, an Elk, and a Shriner; and because so many other JHA members also were Shriners, the sociability run in June 1917 was timed to bring the caravan to Minneapolis at the same time as the national Shriners convention).[4] The evidence was also found in the glad hand and florid speeches, puffed up with literary and historical allusions, proffered by J. D. Clarkson as he made his rounds as advance agent for the JHA; in the grandiloquent speeches befogging the luncheons and nightly banquets hosted in honor of travelers advancing along the highway on the association's many sociability runs; in the high-flown rhetorical style, redolent of real-estate promotions and chamber of commerce boosterism characterizing some of the articles published in the JHA magazines; and in the inspirational poems, such as "The Jefferson Highway Man," also found in those magazines, all representative of the Edgar A. Guest school of versification.

In spite of having great potential for mockery, however, the outlook finding expression in the poems and in some of the activities, speeches, and writings of JHA members may have been precisely what was needed to muster the resolve to take on such a big project as building a 2,300-mile highway—all the more so because the JHA lacked the heavy corporate participation found in the LHA. Or perhaps the expression of that outlook was simply a by-product of the strong sense of self-efficacy and determination to act that motivated the highway's partisans. In any event, many a Johnny-on-the-spot and hustling son-of-a-gun, all of them brimming with pep, stepped forward, and not many years later they had achieved an impressive result.

Although their highway has long sunk beneath the public's recognition or recollection, I've been pleased in recent years to see some indications that that condition seems to be changing. Stirrings of interest in the old "Pine to Palm" highway are evident today in Iowa, Minnesota, Missouri, Kansas, and Oklahoma. In the latter four states, several local museums, libraries, and historical societies are undertaking to identify and collect historical resources related to the highway and its route. The Powers Museum in Carthage, Missouri, has been especially active in this respect, also launching in 2008 a website dedicated to promoting interest in the old highway. Iowa's Department of Transportation also maintains a website providing historical information about the Jefferson Highway. Moreover, the Jefferson Highway is now the subject of historical displays at Itasca State Park in Minnesota; at Colo, Iowa, in the restored and reopened Niland's Café at Reed/Niland

Corner; and at the historical museum in Harrisonville, Missouri. Also, at several places along the Jefferson's route in Missouri, artists have painted elaborate murals celebrating the highway.

Another signal event was the reorganization in March 2011 of the JHA as a Section 501(c)(3) organization dedicated to the promotion, preservation, and study of the Jefferson Highway. The association has since held annual meetings in Iowa, Minnesota, Kansas, Oklahoma, and Missouri and is now within sight of two hundred members, some of whom are very actively engaged in tracking down the highway's history and route in their respective states. Information about joining JHA can be found at the association's website, www.jeffersonhighway.org. The JHA's biggest project to date is a campaign, initiated by and undertaken with Rotary International, to get the highway marked as a "heritage byway" in all of the states through which the highway ran. Success in the trail-marking effort would go a very long way to bring the Jefferson Highway to the attention of the traveling public, and it would also do honor to Hugh Shepard by completing his final thwarted effort to get the highway marked.

Especially helpful now would be accounts of the Jefferson Highway, including accurate route guides, in each of the states through which it ran. I hope that this book, in addition to lifting the highway in Iowa out of the dark night into which it had descended, will prompt others to take on similar books for the other Jefferson Highway states. If this is done, and if the trail-marking project is pursued to completion, then the present JHA will have met the earlier JHA's entreaty, adopted as a resolution in 1928, that "the location and memory of these highways [that is, the Lincoln and the Jefferson] shall be perpetuated to posterity." Certainly that has happened for the Lincoln Highway, and it would now be a well-deserved outcome for the Jefferson Highway as well.

Notes and Sources

PROLOGUE

NOTES

1. American Automobile Association, "Named Highways of the United States," Washington, DC, December 8, 1959, mimeographed.

2. As cited in Earl Swift, *The Big Roads: The Untold Story of the Engineers, Visionaries, and Trailblazers Who Created the American Superhighways* (Boston: Houghton Mifflin Harcourt, 2011), p. 201.

SOURCES

For background information about the "good roads" movement, the era of "named trails," and the subsequent development of the US highway system, the best source is Swift, *The Big Roads*. Other sources that I found useful were three articles by Richard Weingroff published under the general heading "Broader Ribbons across the Land," *Public Roads*, "Special Edition," June 1996, pp. 1–16, 32–33; Tom Lewis, *Divided Highways: Building the Interstate Highways, Transforming American Life* (New York: Viking, 1997); and US Department of Transportation, Federal Highway Administration, *America's Highways, 1776–1976: A History of the Federal Aid Program* (Washington, DC: USDOT, FHA, 1976). The last entry provided information (chapter 3, "Early Federal Aid for Roads and Canals," pp. 16–27) about the National Road, but for a fuller treatment of that topic I turned to Joseph S. Wood, "The Idea of a National Road," in Karl Raitz, ed., *The National Road* (Baltimore: Johns Hopkins University Press, 1996), pp. 93–122.

Other books about the Lincoln Highway have appeared since Drake Hokanson's *The Lincoln Highway: Main Street across America* was published by the University of Iowa Press in 1988, but it remains the best source of information about that earliest successful movement to build a transcontinental automobile highway. Since Hokanson's book was published, books on other named highways have appeared, and in contemplating the writing of a book on the Jefferson Highway, I looked into some of them. Although my book follows a path of organization and presentation different from any of theirs, I found three titles (in addition to Hokanson's) particularly helpful: Max Skidmore, *Moose Crossing: Portland to Portland on the Theodore Roosevelt International Highway* (Lanham, MD: Hamilton Books, 2006); Harold A. Meeks, *On the Road to Yellowstone: The Yellowstone Trail and American Highways, 1900–1930* (Missoula, MT: Pictorial

Histories Publishing, 2000); and Tammy Ingram, *Dixie Highway: Road Building and the Making of the Modern South, 1900–1930* (Chapel Hill: University of North Carolina Press, 2014).

There are no previous books about the Jefferson Highway, and the only articles about that highway that I found are Carol Bohl, "Jefferson Highway: The Palm to Pine Vacation Route of America," *Jackson County [Missouri] Historical Society Journal* 44:1 (Spring 2003): 11–15; Michael F. Jackson, "The Birth of the Jefferson Highway and Its Establishment in Crawford County [Kansas]," a paper written in 1978 in connection with a class on historical research at Pittsburg State University, Pittsburg, Kansas, pp. 1–15 (unpublished but available at the Special Collections Department of Axe Library at Pittsburg State University); and Lyell Henry, "Following in the Lincoln's Wake: The Jefferson Highway," *Lincoln Highway Forum* 15:4 (Summer 2008): 34–46. Much of the content of my article is reprinted in the prologue, chapters 1 and 2, and the epilogue of this book and is used with the permission of the LHA. For granting that permission, I thank Kathy Franzwa, editor of *Lincoln Highway Forum*.

As I note in the text, I could not locate the records of the JHA and am almost certain they no longer exist. However, valuable JHA materials are available in the library of the Iowa Department of Transportation in Ames and in the Special Collections Department of the Iowa State University Library, also in Ames. The Iowa DOT library has registration folders for sixty-four named highways that ran through Iowa, including one for the Jefferson Highway that bulges with correspondence and other items relating to that highway in Iowa from 1915 through 1924. Of course, the library has much other material relevant to the highway, such as early issues of the Iowa State Highway Commission's *Service Bulletin* and photographs, construction plans, and annual reports on road improvement projects. The Iowa State University Library holds the papers of Hugh Shepard, among which is another bulging file containing Shepard's JHA correspondence during 1925 when he was JHA's president. Included in that file are a bound volume of the first year's issues of *Jefferson Highway Declaration* and an ample number of loose later issues of that publication and its successor, the *Modern Highway*.

Here I should also note two other institutions that hold historical materials pertaining to the Jefferson Highway and from which I got some useful items. One is the Powers Museum of Carthage, Missouri, which has taken a lively interest in documenting not only that city's more famous highway—Route 66—but also the less renowned but older road through town, the Jefferson Highway. The other place to be noted is the Special Collections Department of the Leonard H. Axe Library, Pittsburg State University, Pittsburg, Kansas. The latter has the records of the early local JHA organization in Crawford County, Kansas; holds many issues of the JHA magazines (now made available online) and miscellaneous other JHA publications; and is the official repository of the records and proceedings of the revived JHA.

In addition to the previously noted sources of *Jefferson Highway Declaration* and the *Modern Highway*, volumes 1–3 of the former and volumes 4 and 5 of the latter are all available online, and most can be reached through links provided at the website of the JHA (www.jeffersonhighway.org). Volume 3 was also reprinted in 2012 under the title *Jefferson Highway Declaration* by Isha Books of New Delhi, India.

CHAPTER 1

NOTES

1. Much of the content of this chapter is reprinted from Lyell Henry, "Following in the Lincoln's Wake: The Jefferson Highway," *Lincoln Highway Forum* 15:4 (Summer 2008): 34–46. That material is used here with the permission of that publication's editor, Kathy Franzwa, and the LHA.

2. E. T. Meredith, "Linking Up Jefferson's Empire," *Jefferson Highway Declaration*, February 1916, pp. 7–8.

3. E. T. Meredith, "Definite Value of Sociability Run," *Jefferson Highway Declaration*, October 1916, p. 9.

4. Ibid.

5. E. T. Meredith, "The Two Visions," *Jefferson Highway Declaration*, May 1916, pp. 15–16.

6. Walter Lord, *The Good Years* (New York: Harper and Brothers, 1960), p. lx.

7. Reports, Highway Committee, New Orleans Association of Commerce, July 9 and November 12, 1915. I am indebted to John Kelly of the University of New Orleans Library for providing copies of these typed reports.

8. "Highway Association Formed," *Des Moines Register and Leader*, November 16, 1915, p. 3.

9. The key to defeat of the Kansas plan was a decision taken on voting procedure. The Texas and Oklahoma delegations favored votes by individual delegates, which would have given them an advantage, but opponents of the Kansas plan succeeded in getting the conference to adopt a proposal that treated states equally, giving each state four votes. Lafayette Young discussed this and other features of the political struggle at the conference in an article in the November 24, 1915, *Des Moines Leader*.

10. "The Jefferson Highway Meeting," *The Road-Maker*, March 1916, pp. 9–10.

11. E. T. Meredith, "Dollar for Dollar in Roads: How to Get Better Roads without Raising Taxes," *Successful Farming*, August 1916, pp. 10–11, 38–39.

SOURCES

The papers of E. T. Meredith are held in the Special Collections Department of the University of Iowa Library, but I found nothing in them pertaining to Meredith's thoughts about the Jefferson Highway, his role as founder of JHA, or his term as that organization's first president. My guess is that any letters and documents falling under the latter two headings would have been in the JHA office files, which are missing today. Meredith's involvement in the initial JHA meetings in 1915 and 1916, however, I could track through the minutes of those meetings published in *Jefferson Highway Declaration*, as well as in the very substantial coverage of those meetings published in newspapers. I relied on these same sources, as well as articles in the *Road-Maker*, a magazine promoting highway constructions, for forming my descriptions of what took place at those meetings.

For discerning Meredith's thoughts about highways in general and the Jefferson Highway in particular, I found ample evidence in his articles published in *Successful Farming* and *Jefferson Highway Declaration*. For an understanding of Meredith's political involvements, and particularly how his good roads views burdened his 1916 gubernatorial campaign, I turned to Peter L. Petersen, "A Publisher in Politics: Edwin T. Meredith, Progressive Reform, and the Democratic Party, 1912–1928" (PhD diss., University of Iowa, 1971).

About the role of the New Orleans Association of Commerce in calling for a north-south highway through the Mississippi Valley, I found some material in newspaper articles, but a more important source was the official records of that association and its highway committee. For providing copies of relevant association documents, I am indebted to John Kelly, librarian at the University of New Orleans Library, where the New Orleans Association of Commerce archive is located.

CHAPTER 2

NOTES

1. Much of the remainder of this chapter is reprinted from Lyell Henry, "Following in the Lincoln's Wake: The Jefferson Highway," *Lincoln Highway Forum* 15:4 (Summer 2008): 34–46. This material is used here with the permission of that publication's editor, Kathy Franzwa, and the LHA.

2. Any project of planting palm trees along the approach of the Jefferson Highway into New Orleans may soon have been superseded by a larger tree-planting project, if an article appearing in the March 9, 1919, issue of the *Daily Gate City* of Keokuk, Iowa, was accurate. In describing Keokuk's plans to participate in a nationwide campaign to plant trees in honor of American soldiers and sailors killed in World War I, the article included the following: "Louisiana was the first commonwealth to plant trees for the fallen men of that state and is now planting 440 miles of victory oaks along the Jefferson Highway, the principal automobile road of the state."

3. Clarkson believed that sociability runs also demonstrated the potential value of the Jefferson Highway for military purposes, especially in the event of

war ("JH Relay Run as War Measure," *The Road-Maker*, June 1917). On February 6, 1917, he sent the following wire to Secretary of War Newton D. Baker: "In case of war, we tender our Highway and our Highway Organization consisting of 2200 miles of road from Winnipeg to New Orleans and 686 men in our organization located every three or four miles along the Highway. We can touch the button that will put these men in action from Winnipeg to New Orleans. In case of necessity use us to the limit." In his reply the next day, Baker thanked Clarkson "for your generous offer of service" and added that "your communication has been preserved for reference should need arise" ("A Military Road," *Jefferson Highway Declaration*, March 1917).

From Clarkson's point of view, that need did arise once the United States had entered World War I. On May 23, 1917, he wired the director of the Missouri state draft board a proposal to transport eighty-six draftees from Carthage, Missouri, to Camp Dodge, Iowa, via the Jefferson Highway "to demonstrate use of highway for military purposes." The proposal involved using over thirty cars moving in a relay procedure developed in sociability runs and guaranteed delivery within twenty-four hours. Red tape prevented timely approval of the offer, however ("J. H. Offer to Move Troops," *Jefferson Highway Declaration*, June 1918). Clarkson's views about good roads being vital to national defense were sound enough, but how strange it seems today to read about a "tender" of "our Highway" and the volunteer services of JHA for the use of the US government.

4. Walter Parker, letter to Ernest Lee Jahncke, St. Paul, July 24, 1916, included in New Orleans Association of Commerce, Reports of Bureaus, Departments, and Committees, July 1916.

5. Ibid.

6. "Jefferson Highway Directors Meet," *Modern Highway*, January 1922, p. 3.

7. From 1913 through 1925, the Iowa State Highway Commission was directed by law to register named highways within the state upon application and payment of a $5 fee by their promotional organizations. During that period, sixty-four highways were registered. Registration protected the names, colors, signage designs, and routes of the highways against infringement.

SOURCES

Most of this chapter could not have been written save for the plenitude of information available in numerous articles published in newspapers and *Jefferson Highway Declaration*. My reliance on these sources was nearly total for documentation of the early enthusiastic response along the route to the coming of the Jefferson Highway, for biographical data on W. A. Hopkins and Hugh Shepard and their promotion of the Interstate Trail, and for their skilled performances in preparing for the early JHA organizational meetings and securing the incorporation of the Interstate Trail into the Jefferson Highway.

Also getting ample coverage in the previous sources were Clarkson's speeches and activities. Clarkson's presentations to the JHA board of directors, as recorded in the board minutes, were also published in *Jefferson Highway Declaration*. I got some further documentation of Clarkson's life and activities from the Powers Museum in Carthage, Missouri, and for providing this help, I thank Michele Hansford, the now-retired former director of the museum.

Sociability runs, too, got detailed coverage in reports published in *Jefferson Highway Declaration* as well as in newspapers in cities and towns along the route. A summary of all of JHA's sociability runs is presented in Hugh Shepard, "Jefferson Highway Association," *Annals of Iowa*, 3rd ser., 16:6 (October 1928): 432–447. Fred White's letter advising against the January 1926 sociability run is found in the Jefferson Highway registration folder located in the library of the Iowa Department of Transportation. The report containing Walter Parker's description of his participation in the first sociability run comes from the historical file of the New Orleans Association of Commerce, located in the University of New Orleans Library. Once again, my thanks go to librarian John Kelly, this time for retrieving this choice item from that file.

Although newspaper articles yielded some good information about the Saints Highway, the Ayr Line, and the Blue J Route, a more important source of information about the Blue J Route and JHA's efforts to squelch the claim that it was an official variant route of the Jefferson Highway is correspondence found in the Jefferson Highway registration folder on file in the Iowa DOT library.

CHAPTER 3

NOTES

1. Jean C. Prior, *Landforms of Iowa* (Iowa City: University of Iowa Press, 1991), p. 58.

2. Earl Swift, *The Big Roads: The Untold Story of the Engineers, Visionaries, and Trailblazers Who Created the American Superhighways* (Boston: Houghton Mifflin Harcourt, 2011), p. 60.

3. Ibid., p. 74. MacDonald's concept of a federal-aid highway system involving a partnership of state and federal governments prevailed over an alternative plan calling for creation of a national system of highways funded by Congress and administered by a national highway commission. This plan found expression in the Townsend Bill, which was developed in 1919 by Senator Charles Townsend of Michigan and was widely favored by motorists impatient to obtain improved roads. Swift claims that, if it had come to a vote in 1919, it probably would have passed, but its sponsor's constant fiddling with the provisions of the bill delayed its introduction (p. 73). Meanwhile, MacDonald worked assiduously to promote his alternative concept and to enhance the productivity, reputation, and authority of the Bureau of Public Roads.

4. C. C. Clifton, "Authority in Road Building Now Unified," *Des Moines*

Tribune-News, May 16, 1925. This and many more very useful articles written by Clifton I found conveniently brought together in the "Good Roads" Scrapbook Collection located in the State Historical Association of Iowa building in Iowa City.

5. In response to the uneven use by the counties of their bonding power and the consequent inequities and uneven results, Governor John Hammill in 1928 proposed a $100 million state bond issue to fund the building of primary roads in Iowa. Passed by the state legislature in March 1928, the measure was submitted to the voters and passed by a two-to-one majority in the general elections of 1928. The Iowa Supreme Court then declared the bond measure unconstitutional in March 1929. So far as the paving of the Jefferson Highway in Iowa was concerned, however, this outcome didn't much matter, because the paving was already moving ahead by means of the partnership of the state highway commission and affected counties using their bonding authority, as discussed in this chapter.

6. The meaning of "completion" is ambiguous here. Clearly, in Iowa it meant the completion of the paving of the highway across the state. As already noted, however, in Minnesota the highway's paving had not advanced beyond Wadena, although from there north to the Canadian border the route of the Jefferson Highway did have a gravel surface. Perhaps what the monolith really commemorated was the recent completion of the paving of US 65 from the Iowa-Minnesota border to St. Paul and of US 61 from there to Duluth.

SOURCES

For information on the earliest efforts to build the Jefferson Highway, I found an indispensable source to be accounts published in *Jefferson Highway Declaration*, including especially articles reprinted from local newspapers along the route. What had been achieved by 1929 in hard-surfacing the highway is documented in the 1929 JHA route guide, which indicated the road surface— pavement, gravel, or, in a few brief stretches, still no hard surface—at every place along the entirety of the route. In the book cited in the text, geologist Jean Prior presents succinctly and clearly the varying landforms of Iowa that made road building much harder in southern than in northern Iowa.

The best source of information about Thomas MacDonald and his performance both in Iowa and as chief of the Bureau of Public Roads is Swift, *The Big Roads*. Swift also gives a full account of the federal-aid laws of 1916 and 1921 and of the importance of the latter one for laying the foundation of a federal-aid system of interstate highways. For understanding the establishment in 1919 of MacDonald's system of primary and secondary roads in Iowa, I turned to an account published in the Iowa Highway Commission's *Service Bulletin* 7:3–4 (March– April 1919): 6–10, 15. Also useful for supplying some basic facts about the development of highways in Iowa (but lacking the drama and political sense of the presentation found in Swift's pages) is William H. Thompson, *Transportation in Iowa: A Historical Summary* (Ames: Iowa Department of Transportation, 1989).

Finally, some very good items (such as clippings, legislation, pamphlets) relating to the early struggles for improved roads in Iowa repose in the "Good Roads" Scrapbook Collection located in the State Historical Society of Iowa building in Iowa City. I'm indebted to Mary Bennett and other staff members there for making available to me the many folders and pages holding this valuable collection.

CHAPTER 4

NOTES

1. Shepard's JHA presidential file is contained within the Hugh Shepard papers located in the Special Collections Department of the Iowa State University Library in Ames. All quotations from Shepard's correspondence presented in this chapter are taken from items in this file, in each instance indicated by the date of the item cited.

2. Earl Swift, *The Big Roads: The Untold Story of the Engineers, Visionaries, and Trailblazers Who Created the American Superhighways* (Boston: Houghton Mifflin Harcourt, 2011), p. 93.

3. As quoted in Richard F. Weingroff, "From Names to Numbers: The Origins of the US Numbered Highway System," *AASHTO Quarterly* (Spring 1997): 8.

4. From 1916 to 1918, JHA published *Jefferson Highway Declaration*, but in February 1919, for reasons unknown, it ceased publishing that title and began publishing under a new title, the *Modern Highway*. When exactly one year later JHA had joined forces with the association promoting the Pikes Peak Ocean to Ocean Highway, the magazine began to serve the causes of both highways. However, at its annual meeting in January 1923, the JHA decided to end that cooperative arrangement and return to publishing a magazine centered solely on the Jefferson Highway. That latter step was never taken. The reason is unknown, but perhaps it had something to do with Clarkson's departure in 1922. Finding an editor approaching Clarkson's ability to edit a magazine at an acceptable (that is, necessarily low) cost to the JHA would have been difficult. The organization promoting the Pikes Peak Ocean to Ocean Highway continued publishing a magazine but under a new title, the *Appian Way of America*.

5. Shepard apparently had some reservations about the wisdom of opening a new trunk route running through Arkansas. In a letter sent April 23, 1925, to former JHA president A. H. Shafer, Shepard said he had solicited advice on the matter from the Dixie Highway Association (DHA), which had lots of experience with multiple routes. He summarized the reply from DHA as asserting that "the double line highway is most confusing, and that they think that a single line high-

way is a better one, and advise that we keep our highway a single line as far as possible"—in other words, don't add an Arkansas trunk route to the one already existing through Oklahoma and Texas. That this advice came from a Dixie Highway official was ironic, but by then, of course, the Jefferson Highway was also far gone in use of branches and double lines. Moreover, the advice came too late; the decision to add the Arkansas trunk route had already been made in 1924.

6. As quoted in Drake Hokanson, *The Lincoln Highway: Main Street across America* (Iowa City: University of Iowa Press, 1988), p. 109.

7. Hugh Shepard, "Jefferson Highway Association," *Annals of Iowa*, 3rd ser., 16:6 (October 1928): 440.

8. This was the gist of the resolution as summarized by Hugh Shepard in ibid.

SOURCES

My main source of information for this chapter was the file of letters sent by and to Hugh Shepard in connection with the JHA and the Jefferson Highway during Shepard's term as JHA president in 1925. This file, located in the Special Collections Department of the Iowa State University Library in Ames, is a treasure trove of hundreds of letters, all bearing evidence of the problems, issues, and themes that I address in the chapter and without which the chapter could not have been written. Also found in this file are the letters sent by JHA leaders in Louisiana to JHA members there urging the severing of relations with JHA over proposed route changes in Arkansas and Louisiana. Within this file are also a bound volume and some loose issues of *Jefferson Highway Declaration*. For making these indispensable materials available and allowing me to make photocopies of many letters and *Declaration* articles, I tender grateful thanks to the archivists in that department who assisted me.

An excellent source of information about the transition from names to numbers on American interstate highways is, once again, Swift, *The Big Roads*, but for a more detailed account of the steps in that process I turned to Richard F. Weingroff, "From Names to Numbers: The Origins of the US Numbered Highway System," a thirty-one page article available online from the Federal Highway Administration (http://www.fhwa.dot.gov/infrastructure/numbers.cfm). On at least three occasions during the past fifteen years, Richard Weingroff, formerly an information liaison specialist (now retired) with FHA, has provided me with useful information, including a huge stack of photocopied articles on JHA and the Jefferson Highway published in early good roads and trade journals. Most recently, in an e-mail message dated June 4, 2014, he clarified that the Bureau of Public Roads, the Secretary's Joint Committee, and AASHO had no power to compel states to remove the named trail signs; attached to his message were AASHO's "Resolution Five" and the letters exchanged between Thomas Mac-Donald and Senator Earle Mayfield, all cited in this chapter, as well as other documents bearing on the question. My thanks go to him for his kind and indispensable assistance in clearing up a matter about which an incorrect understanding prevails.

For determining the US numbered successor routes to the Jefferson Highway, I used early maps showing both names and numbers, especially an undated *Clason's Touring Atlas* that I could determine from internal evidence probably was published in 1927.

CHAPTER 5

NOTE

1. In the case of Polk County, Des Moines was both the county seat and the state capital.

SOURCES

I began my search for the early Jefferson Highway route by consulting the route of the Interstate Trail as indicated in the county maps and inset maps for principal cities that were published in *Huebinger's Pocket Automobile Guide for Iowa* (Des Moines: Iowa Publishing, 1915). Another helpful item for this purpose was reporter Kristin Buehner's article, "Jefferson Route Can Be Traced," that was prepared with the help of the Iowa DOT and published in the Mason City/Clear Lake *Sunday Globe* on October 22, 1995. For the years following 1919, I could detect changes in the Jefferson's route by consulting the Iowa State Highway Commission's annual road maps of Iowa, all now available online at the Iowa DOT website (http://www.iowadot.gov/maps/msp/historical/transmaps.htm). The Jefferson Highway registration folder available at the Iowa DOT library also has some letters from highway commission officials identifying then-forthcoming route changes.

Leighton Christiansen, Iowa DOT librarian, provided information about the location of Iowa's first automobile fatality occurring south of Hampton, helped me determine the dates and paths of highway route changes at Iowa Falls, and guided me to some Iowa DOT publications having information about the new Oak Street Bridge in Iowa Falls.

As is evident in this chapter's text, I rely heavily on newspaper articles for bits of evidence documenting the impact of the Jefferson Highway on the highway's roadsides and the lives of people living along the highway. More evidence along these lines can often also be found in the National Register of Historic Places registration documents available online at the National Park Service's website (http://www.nps.gov/nR/research; click on "Spreadsheet of NRHP list"). I list here the titles of those I found especially helpful in this respect and include the names of the public historians who did the excellent work of researching and writing the registration documents: "Northwood Central Avenue Historic District"

(Alexa McDowell); "Mason City Downtown Historic District" (Alexa McDowell); "Hampton Double Square Historic District" (Molly Myers Naumann); "Washington Avenue Historic Commercial District [Iowa Falls]" (Molly Myers Naumann); and "The Princess Sweet Shop [Iowa Falls]" (Molly Myers Naumann).

I found very good information on the Park Inn Hotel's history and its restoration in Katherine Haun, *The Historic Park Inn Hotel and City National Bank* (Mason City, IA: Wright on the Park, 2007). Two articles also giving good coverage of the hotel's restoration are Michael Morain, "Wright's Last Hotel Restored," *Des Moines Sunday Register*, September 4, 2011; and "Wright Here in Mason City," *Preservation: The Magazine of the National Trust for Historic Preservation*, Spring 2012, pp. 28–35. For basic information about that other great structure surviving from the Jefferson's earliest days—the Jefferson Highway barn—I relied on "The World of Van-Tine Barns," *Iowa Barn Foundation Magazine* 19:1 (Spring 2013): 3–4.

My knowledge of the history of Reed/Niland Corner in Colo comes from research begun in the 1990s and continued during the time when I was historian on the project of interpretation and restoration there. Most of the information acquired in that research came from many consultations with John and Joan Niland, the last members of the Niland family to own and operate the businesses at Reed/Niland Corner, and from the many photos, clippings, and other documents that they made available to me. For their great help and friendship, I want to convey my gratitude to them here. The history of the businesses at Reed/Niland Corner is recounted in Lyell Henry, "One-Stops on the Lincoln Highway: Four Mid-western Examples," *Lincoln Highway Forum* 5:1 (Fall 1997): 4–15. A very good account of the restoration and reopening of the café and motel is Jim Hill, "Reed/Niland Corner: Restoration and Revival on Two Historic Highways," *SCA Journal* [published by the Society for Commercial Archeology] 32:1 (Spring 2014): 14–21.

About the other two vintage motels on the Jefferson route, much of what I know and relate in my text also came from talks with present or recent owners— Debra Luedtke, co-owner with her husband, Daniel, of the Royal Motel in Northwood; and Terry and Deb Super, the recently retired former owners of the Scenic Inn in Iowa Falls. I'm even further in debt to Debra Luedtke for passing on to me a seven-page unpublished narrative, "The Royal Motel's History," written by previous owners Kathy and Larry Richards in 1995. In the case of the Scenic Inn, I found a substantial amount of newspaper coverage of its earlier iteration as the Scenic City Motel and, before that, the Scenic City Kabin Kamp. Information about the earliest days of the "kabin kamp" comes from Frank Gruber, "Log Cabin Tourist Camp Proves Profitable to Mrs. Zetta Thompson," *Wayside Salesman*, February 1931, pp. 7, 26.

What little I know about wind farming in Iowa and its varying presence along the route of the Jefferson Highway I got from Bob Ausberger, an advocate of wind power and practitioner of no-till farming near Jefferson, Iowa, and from articles and data available online from various sources. Information about Chapin's once-brighter days commercially I got from a spiral-bound booklet: Burnice Greimann, *The Chapin Story: 140 Years of History, 1857–1997* (Hampton, IA: Pronto Print, 1997). Finally, for helping me learn more about Manly's earlier days of greatness as a major hub of the Rock Island Railroad; for loaning me his copy of a special January 7, 1915, edition of the *Manly Chief* that reviewed the big local impact of that occurrence; and for giving me a sneak preview of the railroading museum that he and his two uncles were preparing to open, I here offer my thanks to Brad Sabin.

CHAPTER 6

NOTES

1. Of course, construction of a full cloverleaf interchange would have required use of the northeast quadrant on which Margaret Hicks's house was situated, but the highway commission made no move to secure that land. Doubtless, all the commission sought to do at that time was build a more limited interchange, one that still required cars to cross the path of opposing traffic and to stop when transiting from one highway to the other. It seems plausible, however, that the commission had plans for eventual construction of a cloverleaf interchange or at least wanted to keep that option open. That would explain why the commission introduced the cloverleaf concept into the court trial, sought all of the land in the two quadrants south of US 30 (and Reed's property in the northwest quadrant as well), and succeeded in persuading both courts that, save for the "rounding" obstacle, the commission should have control over all of the land bordering that intersection.

2. Nevada Historical Preservation Commission, "A Historic Walking Tour down Main Street of Nevada, Iowa!" This is a two-sided glossy brochure describing and depicting in colored photos significant buildings in Nevada's commercial district. More information about the Story Hotel is available in the document supporting the listing (May 9, 2003) of the Downtown Historical District in the National Register of Historic Places. Although that document is partially developed in terms of the impact of the rising use of the private automobile in the early twentieth century, no mention is made of the Jefferson Highway as the "other" interstate highway that once ran through Nevada.

3. Later the Des Moines Chamber of Commerce and Greater Des Moines Committee were merged in the Greater Des Moines Chamber of Commerce, whose early papers are held in the Greater Des Moines Chamber of Commerce collection located in the Special Collections Department of the University of Iowa Library. Unfortunately, I was unsuccessful in finding anything in that collection that could amplify the information in the newspaper stories cited in the

text. Indeed, I found very little else there bearing on early highways through Des Moines.

SOURCES

My principal sources for determining the original Jefferson Highway route from Colo to Des Moines and for tracing the subsequent changes in the route were the same as those indicated in chapter 5—early Huebinger county road maps, annual highway commission road maps, and materials in the Jefferson Highway registration folder in the Iowa DOT library. The contest between the original route from Nevada to Ankeny and the final route running by way of Ames got considerable coverage in newspaper articles, as did Parley Sheldon's heavy part in promoting the latter route. I found more information on Sheldon's activities in minutes of JHA meetings published in *Jefferson Highway Declaration* and in the Iowa DOT library's Jefferson Highway registration folder. Using newspaper articles and inset maps of Des Moines in early road guides, I was able to determine successive changes of the highway's route through Des Moines.

The issues involved in Charlie Reed's tangle with the highway commission are set forth in Judge Henderson's February 20, 1935, decree in *Reed v. Iowa State Highway Commission et al.* and in the Iowa Supreme Court's March 17, 1936, opinion under the same name affirming the decision of the lower court. I'm grateful to Dorian Myhre, judicial specialist at the Story County Courthouse, for retrieving and copying for me the lower-court decree stored there on microfilm and to Jan Olive Full for securing a copy of the Iowa Supreme Court's opinion for me. Very full coverage of this case can also be found in Annette Murnan, "Reed's Complex Was in Jeopardy," *Nevada [Iowa] Journal*, August 17, 1988, p. 85. At the county courthouse in Nevada I obtained the list of exhibits, the first two of which indicated the highway commission's interest in advanced highway interchange designs, including the cloverleaf. John Niland provided a copy of the February 2, 1935, letter that Charlie Reed received from his lawyer revealing that the highway commission had designs on also acquiring Reed's property in the northwest quadrant of the intersection of the two highways. In 2001, while doing research for the interpretive work at the Reed/Niland Corner restoration project, I asked staff members in Iowa DOT's Records Management Department to look for evidence of what the highway commission's long-range plans for Reed/Niland Corner might have been. In spite of their good efforts, they located nothing.

In its *Annual Report* for 1916, the Iowa highway commission announced its intention to build the underpass and replace the viaduct near the intersection of the highway, creek, and two railroad lines west of Colo. Its 1918 *Annual Report* brought the news that the underpass was done but that World War I had forced the deferral of the other project. Copies of all annual reports of the Iowa highway commission are available in the Iowa DOT library. A good brief discussion of the history and physical features of the setting of the approximately 5-mile segment of County Road E41 (formerly the Lincoln and the Jefferson Highways) reaching from the grade separation at the northeast border of Colo to the west end of the present overpass crossing creek and railroad lines is Jan Olive Nash (now Jan Olive Full), *Intensive Historical Survey of the I-Beam Bridge over Dye Creek*, a report submitted to the Story County engineer in August 2000. Although she found the subject I-beam bridge to be a contributing part of a district eligible for listing in the National Register of Historic Places, the bridge is no longer there, nor are several other significant roadside features noted in her report.

CHAPTER 7

NOTES

1. Lowell Soike, "Viewing Iowa's Farmsteads," in Robert F. Sayre, ed., *Take This Exit: Rediscovering the Iowa Landscape* (Ames: Iowa State University Press, 1989), pp. 153–172. For per capita income data for Iowa counties, I consulted "Annual Per Capita Personal Income," a table compiled by the Iowa Community Indicators Program at Iowa State University and available online (http://www.icip.iastate.edu/tables/income/per-capita-income). Data based on other measures, such as median family income, are also available at other sites online (for instance, http://www.iowadatacenter.org) and usually show Clarke and Decatur falling significantly below the other seven Jefferson Highway counties.

2. *Iowa: A Guide to the Hawkeye State*, compiled and written by the Federal Writers' Project of the Works Progress Administration for the State of Iowa, American Guide Series (New York: Viking Press, 1938), p. 390.

3. On this occasion, Shepard's tune was different from that of four years earlier. While serving as JHA president in 1925, Shepard had reacted to criticism of Iowa's automobile roads published in a Des Moines newspaper by claiming that the roads were fine in northern Iowa but that the southern counties were laggard in road improvements. The editor of the *Osceola Sentinel* took offense, noting accurately that residents of the southern counties were steadily committed to improving the Jefferson Highway but that the costs and the difficulties of doing so were far greater there than in the northern counties ("We Don't Like His Criticisms of Our Roads," August 20, 1925).

4. The other bridge is a concrete deck girder bridge over the Winnebago River north of Mason City on US 65. Built in 1926, it was placed on the National Register of Historic Places in 1998. Two other historic bridges are found on later routes of the Jefferson Highway: a 1934 steel stringer bridge over Squaw Creek on US 65 at Hampton, and a 1913 concrete arch bridge over Walnut Creek on US 69 halfway between Ames and Huxley. All information about bridges cited here comes from the detailed listings found at www.bridgehunter.com.

5. That "veritable sea of mud" actually continued for only a couple of miles, be-

yond which US 69 mostly had a concrete or gravel surface all the way to Kansas City.

SOURCES

For identification of most of the early route from Des Moines to the Missouri border, I drew on the same sources specified in my discussion of sources for chapters 5 and 6 along with others. I found the route through Summerset conveniently described in *A Short History of Summerset, Iowa*, a booklet compiled in 2012 by Jerry Beatty, a member of the Warren County Historical Society, which provided the booklet. From Loring Miller, longtime resident of Leon and active member of the Decatur County Historical Society, I learned the highway's early route through Leon. (He is also the Rotary official spearheading that organization's campaign to put up signs marking the Jefferson Highway as a "heritage byway.") For information bearing on the original route through Medora and the later route change there, I drew on newspaper accounts; materials in the Jefferson Highway registration folder in the Iowa DOT library; and Fred White's letter to Hugh Shepard, found in the Shepard papers in the Iowa State University Library, discussing plans for "the famous Medora link." Finally, I am indebted to Leighton Christiansen, Iowa DOT librarian, for determining the dates of the construction of the pony truss bridge on Old US 69, the relocation of US 69 from that original road, and the abandonment of the highway segments south of Indianola. Further information about the pony truss bridge I got from www .bridgehunter.com.

From the documentation prepared for their listings in the National Register of Historic Places, I obtained useful information about the county courthouses located on the Jefferson's route in Indianola and Leon. In an e-mail message sent in reply to my inquiry, Marie White, an active member of the Clarke County Historical Society, told me more about the circumstances leading to the replacement in 1956 of the old Clarke County Courthouse in Osceola than I learned at the county's website. I'm also greatly indebted to her for locating some choice photos of Jefferson Highway scenes in Osceola and for helping me connect to the scanned Osceola newspapers available online at the Osceola Public Library's website (http://osceola.advantage-preservation.com).

The basic facts about the Hastie station located between Des Moines and Indianola come from a one-page information sheet prepared by the Warren County Historic Preservation Commission and available at the station. For information on the Jefferson Highway's brief intersection and overlap of the Mormon Pioneer Trail, I consulted *The Mormon Pioneer Trail across Iowa in 1846*, a booklet prepared in 2006 by the National Park Service as an "auto tour route interpretive guide." This booklet and similar guides for the Mormon Trail in other states are available at no charge from the National Park Service.

NOTES

1. A small portion of this epilogue is reprinted from Lyell Henry, "Following in the Lincoln's Wake: The Jefferson Highway," *Lincoln Highway Forum* 15:4 (Summer 2008): 34–46. It is used here with the permission of that publication's editor, Kathy Franzwa, and the LHA.

2. Wingo's expedition received coverage in many newspapers, but the most convenient sources of information about it and him are Gene Fowler, *Mavericks: A Gallery of Texas Characters* (Austin: University of Texas Press, 2008), pp. 61–64, and Wingo's own account, *Around the World Backwards* (Austin, TX: Eakin Press, 1982). In his book, Wingo doesn't indicate by highway name or number the route that he followed from Dallas to Joplin. However, all of the many intermediary towns and cities that he acknowledges reaching on the way make it virtually certain that he traveled the Jefferson Highway route, which was then known as US 73, but today as US 69.

3. The citations for these four walking expeditions are, respectively, "Canadian Youths Will Walk to New Orleans," *Cedar Rapids Evening Gazette*, October 17, 1914; "He Is Walking the Jefferson Highway," *Pocahontas [Iowa] Democrat* (reprinted from the *Osceola Tribune*), May 8, 1924; [no title], *Jefferson [Iowa] Bee*, January 4, 1922; and "Boys Will Walk from Iowa to Calif. as Road Boosters," *Des Moines Daily News*, May 18, 1914.

4. Shepard's memberships in these specific fraternal lodges are indicated in a cartoon drawing of Shepard and his various affiliations published in the *Mason City Globe-Gazette* on February 24, 1916. The coordination of schedules of the sociability run and Shriners convention was reported in "Osceola Is One of Night Controls," *Osceola Democrat*, March 15, 1917.

SOURCES

Tourist court and motel associations, oil companies, and other organizations doing business along the highways once published listings of highway hostelries classified by state and city and sometimes by highway. I have a large number of these listings, and from them I was able to discern the growth of private tourist accommodations along the Jefferson Highway in the late 1920s and throughout the 1930s. For data on the free tourist camps along the highway in the early 1920s, my main source was a tourist camp booklet published in 1923 by JHA, but additional information came from newspaper articles. My comments about Green Gable camps and their significance as the original attempt to build a nationwide cabin camp chain are based on research presented in Lyell Henry, "'From Coast to Coast, They're Springing Up': Green Gable Cabin Camps," *SCA Journal* [published by Society for Commercial Archeology] 31:1 (Spring 2013): 8–15.

For information about the availability (or lack thereof) of travel accommodations for persons of color on the highways, I consulted five annual issues of *The Negro Motorist Green Book* and five similar specialized guidebooks, all issued between 1938 and 1964, and also drew on earlier research presented in the following: Lyell Henry, "Accommodations 'For Colored,'" *SCA Journal* [published by Society for Commercial Archeology] 23:2 (Fall 2005), 4–11; Lyell Henry, "Serving All Travelers on the Lincoln Highway: Motel Sepia of Cedar Rapids, Iowa," *Lincoln Highway Forum*, 7:2&3 (Spring/Summer 2000), 14–18; and Lyell Henry, "George Washington Carver Did *NOT* Sleep Here!," an unpublished investigation of public accommodations for African American travelers on the Lincoln Highway.

I found documentation of the close connection between the blazing of the Jefferson Highway in Minnesota and the formation of the Ten Thousand Lakes Association in that association's first promotional booklet, *The Land of Ten Thousand Lakes over the Jefferson Highway in Minnesota* (1919), a copy of which I own. For an account of how the Jefferson Highway in Minnesota also gave rise to a bus company, see Margaret Walsh, "Minnesota's 'Mr. Bus': Edgar F. Zelle and the Jefferson Highway Transportation Company," *Minnesota History* (Winter 1991): 307–322.

What first caused me to think of the early automobile highways as stages calling forth new kinds of performances were the postcards issued by so many of the early zany travelers along those highways. I now have a collection of about 180 of those postcards. Although none in my collection specifically cites travel on the Jefferson Highway, the very abundance of postcards of this kind prompted me to look for documentation of such travel in the newspaper archives. Pursuing this line of inquiry also eventually led me to Plennie Wingo's book and, thereafter by sheer good luck, to photos of Wingo offered at auction on eBay.

Sources of information about the Jefferson Highway that I mention in this chapter include three that can be tapped online: the Iowa DOT, for information about the Jefferson Highway and the Interstate Trail, www.iowadot.gov /autotrails/jeffersoninterstate5.aspx; Special Collections, Pittsburg State University, Pittsburg, Kansas (JHA's official archive), for historic publications and other materials about the Jefferson Highway, http://axedigital.pittstate.edu /cdm/landingpage/collection/jeffhway; and the Jefferson Highway Association, for information about the JHA and activities along the highway today, www .jeffersonhighway.org, which also includes links to maps tracing the JH route through Iowa and some of the other states. The JHA publishes a quarterly newsletter under the revived title of *Jefferson Highway Declaration*, but it is available to members only.

Index

Note: Page numbers in *italics* refer to illustrations.

Huebinger's Pocket Automobile Guide for Iowa, 108
Huemann-Kelly, Sandii, 112, *112*
Humboldt [Iowa] Republican, 137
Humboldt Independent, 150
Humeston [Iowa] New Era, 172
Huxley, Iowa, 132

Illinois Central depot, 97
Indianola, Iowa, 142–143; abandoned road near, *144,* 165; and bootlegging, 169; and Interstate Trail, 145; lodging in, 174, 176; and US 65/US 69, 139
Indianola Herald, 141
Interstate 35 (I-35), 167, 176
Interstate Trail, 37–39; condition of, 44, 47–48; Iowa's construction of, 7; leadership behind, 35–36; and Osceola, Iowa, 145; and route of Jefferson Highway, 18–19; and terrain of Iowa, 49; walking expeditions on, 170, 172
Interstate Trail Association: and condition of roads, 48; and Jefferson Highway Association, 35, 37; leadership of, 39; and route of highway, 145
Iowa: and bond issuance, 42–43, 55, 56, 187n5; capitol building of, 132, 133, *133*; as context for investigation, 7; as crossroads of Jefferson and Lincoln highways, 13; enthusiasm for Jefferson Highway in, 25; fund raising in, 25; highway numbers in, 72; interest in highway in, 179–180; and Interstate Trail, 37, 47–48; and interstate-span of highway, 4, *21*; and Iowa Primary Road No. 1, 60; and Jefferson Highway Association, 180; landscape of, 48–49; and Minnesota border,

77; and Missouri border, 164; and monument to highway, 56–57, *58,* 59; and Panama-Pacific Exposition in San Francisco, 36–37; paving in, 46, 47; primary and secondary roads in, 51–52; primary road development fund of, 53–54, 55; road conditions in, 48, 84, 137–138, 140, 164, 194n3; and route of Jefferson Highway, 17–18, 39; Southern Pasture region of, 138; taxes in, 53. *See also specific cities and towns*
Iowa Community Visioning Program, 83
Iowa Department of Transportation (DOT), 6, 101, 114, 179
Iowa Falls, Iowa, 97–103, *99, 102,* 165, 176
Iowa Falls Community Club, 100
Iowa Good Roads Association, 38
Iowa Northern Railroad, 83
Iowa Primary Road No. 1, 60, 100, 131, 167
Iowa Recorder, 134
Iowa State Capitol Building, 132, *133,* 133
Iowa State College (now University), 131
Iowa State Highway Commission: on accidents on highways, 168–169; as advocate for road improvements, *8*; and Ames–Des Moines road, 131–132; authority of, 50; and Blue J Highway, 39; and county-level road construction, 50–51; and federal aid, 51, 52, 53; and interchange proposal in Story County, 115–121, 192n1; and Jefferson Highway Association, 61–62, 64; leadership of (*see* MacDonald, Thomas H.; White, Fred); and Medora's roads, 148; and numbering of highways,

180; implementation of, 29–30, *31*; Jefferson Highway Association's plans for, 61–62, 64–65, *66*, 67, 70–71; and numbering system, 71–72; and "Pine to Palm" slogan, 30, *31*, 152; and state directors' responsibilities, 40; and trail associations, 62–64

Mason City, Iowa, 85–91; and Dillinger gang bank robbery, 169; lodging in, 85, 87–89, *88*, 114, 166, 174; paving in, *86*; road conditions in, 84; and US 65, 85, 87, 91, 165

Mason City Globe-Gazette: on Dillinger gang, 83; on gala event, 90; on Hubbard's appeal, 106; on road conditions, 84, 137; on route of highway, 91; on Shepard, 37, 137, 164; on US Highway No. 65 Association's meeting, 74

Mayfield, Earle, 63

McIninch, George, 57, 73

Medora, Iowa: hilly terrain of, *147*; road improvements in, 146, 148–150; and route of Jefferson Highway, 145, *149*, 165

Medora Store, Medora, Iowa, 146

Memorial Hall, Hampton, Iowa, 96

Memorial Hall, Sheffield, Iowa, *94*

Mencken, H. L., 178

Men's Garden Club of Des Moines, 142

Meredith, Edwin T.: as advocate for road improvements, *12*, 11–16; on allure of travel, 170; and Clarkson, 22, 27, 28, 34; and Des Moines route, 136; on economic benefits of highway, 26; on funding the construction, 42–43; on goals for completion, 44; and leadership of the JHA, 17, 18, 22, 39, 177; and

Lincoln Highway, 11, 22; political ambitions of, 22, 24, 26; records of, 183–184; two visions of, 14–15, 27, 28

Meredith Publications, 11

Meridian Highway, 5

Middle River, 141

military preparedness, 15, 184n3

Minnesota: hard-surfaced roads in, 46; highway numbers in, 72; interest in highway in, 179; and interstate tourism, 25–26; and Interstate Trail, 37; and interstate-span of highway, 4, *21*, *23*; and Iowa border, 77; and Jefferson Highway Association, 180; modern highways in, 167; and monument to highway, *56–57*, *58*; paving in, 46, 47, 56, 187n6; and route of Jefferson Highway, 17–19, 39; and vacation tourism, 168

Minnesota Scenic Highway, 20, 22

Minnesota State Highway Commission, 25

Mississippi River Scenic Highway, 4, 39

Mississippi Valley, 13

Mississippi Valley Highway, 4

Missouri: enthusiasm for Jefferson Highway in, 25; hard-surfaced roads in, 46; highway numbers in, 72; interest in highway in, 179–180; and Interstate Trail, 37, 47; and interstate-span of highway, 4, *21*, *23*; Iowa's border with, 164; and Jefferson Highway Association, 180; modern highways in, 167; paving in, 47; and route of Jefferson Highway, 17–19, 22; volunteer labor in, 45–46

Modern Highway: on French's quali-

and Grant Highway, 98; and
Hampton, 97; and Hastie Gas Station, *140*; and highway markers,
110; and Hubbard, 103, 104, 105;
incorporation of Jefferson Highway, viii, 56, 165; and Indianola,
139, 142, 143, 144–145; and Interstate Trail, 145; and Iowa Falls, 96,
98, 100–102, 103, 165; and Kensett, 80–81; and lodging, 176; and
Mason City, 85, 87, 91; and Minnesota-Iowa border, 77; and Nevada,
76; and Northwood, 77, 79; paving
of, 187n6; range covered by, 76;
and Rockwell cutoff, 91; and route
changes, 75, 165–166; and route
controversies, 74; and Sheffield,
92–93, 95; speed limit on, 165, 166;
and Story County, 107; and Story
County interchange proposal, 116–
121, *120*; and Summerset, 140–142;
and US Highway No. 65 Association, 74; and Zearing, 107–108, 109
US 69: and Ankeny, 130, 132; and
Cool, 146; and Davis City, 160, 162,
163; and Decatur County line, *155*;
and Des Moines, 132, 134, 136; and
Hastie Gas Station, *140*; hilly terrain of, 146; and Huxley, 132; incorporation of Jefferson Highway,
viii, 56, 165; and Indianola, 139,
142, 143, 144–145; and Interstate
Trail, 145; and Lamoni, 162, 163,
164; and Leon, 157, *158*, *161*; and
Liberty, 151; and Medora, 149; and
Osceola, 145, 151, 152, *153*, *154*, *155*;
range covered by, 76; and route
changes, 75; speed limit on, 165;
and Summerset, 140–142
US Army, 15
US Congress, 2, 53, 186n3

US Highway No. 65 Association, 74
US Navy, 15

vacation travel, 25–26, 30, 168
Van Wert, Iowa, 156–157, *157*
viaduct near Colo, Iowa, 121–124, *123*,
124
volunteers, road building of, 42

Wade's Café, 153
walking expeditions, 170, *171*, 172,
196n2
Walters, C. E., 117
wanderlust, 169–170
Warren County, 139–150; courthouse
of, 143; and Interstate Trail, 145;
landscape of, 138; road conditions
in, 140, 164
Warren County Board of Supervisors,
148
Warren County Conservation Commission, 150
Warren County Historic Preservation
Commission, 139
Washington Post, 9
*Waterloo [Iowa] Evening Courier and
Reporter*, 39
Waterloo Evening Courier, 92
Watts service station, Northwood,
Iowa, 79–80
Waubonsie Trail, 36
Wayne County, 145
W. C. Bagg Camp, Osceola, Iowa, 174
Weldon, Iowa, 153, 155–156
White, Fred: and building the highway, 56; chief engineer appointment of, *54*, 54–55; and markers for highway, 61–62, 64; on
Medora's roads, 148; and monument to highway, 57; and numbering of highways, 61–62; and paving

The Archaeological Guide to Iowa
By William E. Whittaker, Lynn M. Alex,
and Mary De La Garza

Carnival in the Countryside:
The History of the Iowa State Fair
By Chris Rasmussen

The Drake Relays:
America's Athletic Classic
By David Peterson

Dubuque's Forgotten Cemetery:
Excavating a Nineteenth-Century Burial Ground
in a Twenty-First-Century City
By Robin M. Lillie and Jennifer E. Mack

Duffy's Iowa Caucus Cartoons:
Watch 'Em Run
By Brian Duffy

Equal before the Law:
How Iowa Led Americans to Marriage Equality
By Tom Witosky and Marc Hansen

Iowa Past to Present:
The People and the Prairie,
Revised Third Edition
By Dorothy Schwieder, Thomas Morain,
and Lynn Nielsen

The Iowa State Fair
By Kurt Ullrich

The Lost Region:
Toward a Revival of Midwestern History
By Jon K. Lauck

Main Street Public Library:
Community Places and Reading Spaces
in the Rural Heartland, 1876–1956
By Wayne A. Wiegand

Necessary Courage:
Iowa's Underground Railroad
in the Struggle against Slavery
By Lowell Soike

On Behalf of the Family Farm:
Iowa Farm Women's Activism since 1945
By Jenny Barker Devine

A Store Almost in Sight:
The Economic Transformation of Missouri
from the Louisiana Purchase to the Civil War
By Jeff Bremer

Transcendental Meditation in America:
How a New Age Movement Remade a Small Town in Iowa
By Joseph Weber

What Happens Next?
Essays on Matters of Life and Death
By Douglas Bauer